The Secret
to
Everyday
Communication

(Without Argument)

A WISE OWL BOOK

Acknowledgments

Writing this book has been far from a solo journey. I want to give my thanks to the many people who shared their time, expertise, friendship, love, and ongoing support:

The brilliant Peer Reviewers who offered their precious time reading the manuscript, sharing their observations, and strengthening the content. Thanks to Rachelle Herdman, Cynthia Johnson, George Lynn, Moonwater, and Harlan Weniger.

With numerous books of his own, my brother Dennis Ortman clearly articulated his secrets to writing when needed most.

Jinine Martin patiently read the rewritten versions of this book and encouraged me with her grace throughout the journey.

My friend Bob Lanphear for his far-reaching vision and creative elegance, bringing a sense of proportion to the cover design and text.

My gifted, gracious, and witty editor, Susan Pohlman, who polished my writing into readable words, helping me say what I mean more clearly.

My lifelong friends, William Spitzley and Alex Campbell, for their encouragement and insights throughout our friendship.

The thousands of students and clients who kept me inspired with their presence, commitment, and stories throughout the decades.

Kristen Chandler, my loving partner who was there as my sounding board, helping me organize my abstract ideas into concrete thoughts. I want to thank her for being flexible and accommodating during the long hours spent at my desk writing. This project would not have happened without her encouragement and belief in me.

Finally, in remembrance of my wise mentor, Al West (1915-2010), who led me to pursue answers to life's critical questions. I am ever grateful for his generosity and foresight.

Contents

Introduction

*Competition is the law of the jungle, but
cooperation is the law of civilization.* - Peter Kropotkin

My mentor of many years shared with me, *"We are like movie projectors; we project our feelings, needs, desires, perspective and attitudes onto everyone we meet."* The projector ran non-stop in our household, growing up in a family of five boys. When two or more entered a room, an argument often ensued. *"I want to watch my TV show!" "No, it's my turn to choose!"*… and so forth. Mom would rush to the rescue and continually remind us of her frustration, *"I wish you boys would just get along and not fight!"* Unfortunately, no one ever taught us **HOW**.

Every day, we dance among the differences of what **I** want versus what **you** want. Someone makes a mistake, and we criticize them. Our partner is being controlling, so we shut down. Our children's wants are persistent, and we endlessly repeat, *"I said no!"* Our defiant teenager will not listen, so we take away privileges. Our co-workers stack us with their responsibilities. We complain to closed ears. Our boss rides us relentlessly and on and on. We could settle these circumstances by responding differently.

Marcus Tullius Cicero, a Roman philosopher who lived more than two thousand years ago, said, *"We live in an age of disagreement."* His words still apply today. Discord isn't going away anytime soon. We may prefer to reside in the cozy corner of our emotional palette, but, human interaction guarantees a broader spectrum of emotional experiences. Apart from extreme poverty or severe illness, most human distress stems from problematic relationships.

When disagreement escalates into an argument, communication takes on a whole new demeanor. We hear untrue assessments and words weaponized to hurt—all to prove one's point. We walk away stewing, not getting our *say* or *way*. We are not going to get along with everyone we encounter. We each have our threshold of tolerance.

The passions of human nature do not change. Five thousand years ago, a mother mourned the death of her child. Today, the same. Defying human nature is a losing proposition. *Emotions, competition, pride, desire, self-interest, ego,* (and of course, *love*) are human instincts. Best we learn to navigate and respond to this interpersonal terrain skillfully.

Why This Book

Each school of martial arts has a different philosophy. Some strike first when threatened, favoring offense. Others emphasize a strong foundation that patiently absorbs or deflects the initial attack, then responds using the opponent's momentum to their advantage. Communication is similar in many ways.

This book's approach is a blend of both an *enlightened* defense and a *straightforward* offense. We must ***first*** realize it serves our interest to *get out of our way* to get *our way*—a paradox of sorts. A calm view has a clear vantage point.

It is far easier for us to change a person's perspective than try to change their character. As a mediator, people would often ask me to explain the process. I would respond with an analogy: *"It is like walking into a room with both parties wearing a paper bag over their head with just one small hole in which they view the situation. My role is to skillfully punch holes in the bag to allow them to see the bigger picture and make a better choice."* When we help expand a person's perspective of the situation, different choices and actions often follow. My experience led to the creation of the A.C.T. Way to Communicate.

I developed and refined the three skills of the A.C.T. over a three and a half decade career in communication as a coach, mediator and trainer. I had the luxury of listening to more than 24,000 stories and admissions shared by students and clients. The tales told of the problems faced in everyday communication at work and home.

Patterns emerged. The most reoccurring issues were:

- **Arguing** or **Pressuring** to get our way without listening.
  (Unable to accept "no" for an answer. Badger.)

- **Assuming** we know what others are thinking and feeling.
  (Acting upon false conclusions without verifying.)

- **Forcing our Ideas** without considering the needs of others.
  (One person's needs dominate.)

All three ploys resulted in the same outcome—resistance or accommodation with growing *resentment*. Over time, the relationship would suffer. Imagine how our interaction would differ if we felt our **voice** was **heard,** our **dignity** was **respected,** and our **interests** and **needs** were taken into account? The A.C.T. skills can help advance these outcomes.

Getting Our A.C.T. Together

Everyday communication works, until it doesn't. The A.C.T. Way to Communicate is an approach that moves *with*, not *against*, the instincts of human nature. We learn to offset *arguing, assumptions*, or *forced ideas* respectfully and take steps to discuss what we want without resorting to such impulses. Conversation becomes more open, fair, and less emotional. The three skills of the A.C.T. Way are: *Acknowledge, Clarify,* and *Talk.*

The A.C.T. Way to Respond to Everyday Communication Without Argument

Acknowledge	Clarify	Talk

Emotional ———————————————— Conversational

Emotional Zone	Discovery Zone	Discussion Zone

Strong emotions compromise the ability to reason and listen.

Copyright © 2021 Mark Ortman

1 We **Acknowledge** to create a conducive atmosphere for listening when *emotions* are present. Strong emotions compromise the ability to reason and listen.

2 We **Clarify** by asking the right questions to hear what the other person means and wants. Discover and understand their version before sharing ours opens two-way listening.

3 We **Talk**, discuss, or negotiate what we want from a more informed position, making conversation easier.

The A.C.T. skills can be used in *sequence*, or *freely*, and apply to all interactions, written or spoken. These three skills invite *discussion* over an *argument* in the many interpersonal challenges endemic in today's world.

Communication is how we interact and socialize, yet our educational system neglects to teach these needed skills. I wrote this book because I am not exempt from the challenges of human nature. I am continually learning and growing. I want a practical interpersonal guide to remind the reader (and myself) what works and what doesn't and *how* and *why* it works in everyday communication.

This thin volume is packed with examples, insights, tips, and stories. The book is organized into three parts, sixteen chapters, and fifty-two sections covering many real-life scenarios. Re-read and highlight the skills most helpful to you. Use the book as a reference to become more confident handling those challenging conversations encountered at home, or work. I hope this book will enrich your daily interactions and relationships in today's changing world.

Mark Ortman

PART ONE
Acknowledge

The A.C.T. Way to Respond to Everyday Communication Without Argument

Acknowledge   Clarify   Talk

Emotional   Conversational

Emotional Zone
Calm emotions by validating their experience to let them know they were heard.

Discovery Zone   Discussion Zone

Strong emotions compromise the ability to reason and listen.

The Meaning Behind Words

When people speak, there is far more to what they say than what we hear. When we listen <u>*carefully*</u>, we tune in to the speaker's interests, emotions, values, and needs behind their words.

The diagram below defines the levels of listening behind what people say they *want*, must *have*, or won't *do*.

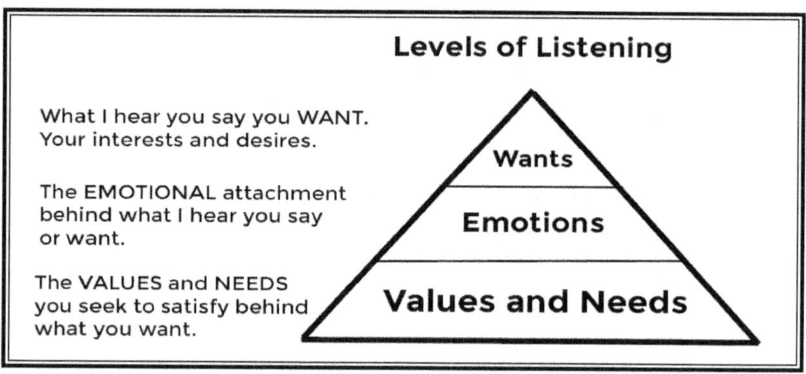

Let's review the three levels of listening and their influence in everyday communication, starting with the *Wants* level and working down the triangle.

What I WANT

What we perceive we lack, we *want*. We tie our desires and interests into what we express. The *Wants* level is where we hear people voice their requests, complaints, advice, ideas, criticism, or judgments. When we agree, we work toward accommodating. If we disagree, it is easy to get stuck at the *Wants* level arguing over what was said, who did what to whom, or who is right. We go over the issue again and again.

Instead, it is useful to note which levels (Emotions, Values or Needs) are *guiding* their words before we react. Then, we can understand the <u>importance</u> of the meaning behind what was said. Acknowledging the emotion or the actual values/need demonstrates we're *genuinely* listening. Doing so, emotions relax to ask questions to clarify (Part 2) and open a discussion (Part 3).

EMOTIONS Within the Words

The tongue has no bones but is strong enough to break a heart. - Irina Swart

Emotions are hard-wired into our being. No matter how smart or clever we are, no one can prevent feelings from being experienced, especially in times of perceived threat. What I say I want has a relationship to what I feel. *"I want to eat because I'm hungry." "I'm going to get some exercise because I'm stressed out." "I'm overwhelmed with work and want uninterrupted time to finish."* Emotions play a fundamental role in our actions and words, whether evident or not. **If it didn't matter emotionally, we wouldn't care.**

Our daily interactions are not always straightforward. People can harbor many things behind a happy facade—home or work pressures, a lousy mood, frustrations, stresses, or issues from a painful past that have little to do with us until triggered. What is going on behind the scenes colors the tone of our exchange.

In a meeting, Emma appears upset about something. Her curt tone sounds like she's angry with me, even though there is no reason to be. Something is off-kilter about our interaction. To find out, I acknowledge her experience. "I'm sensing you are upset about something, Emma." I learn she is upset about a personal matter and didn't mean to take her frustration out on me. She apologizes. The atmosphere shifts as her emotions relax.

TIP: The <u>context</u> of the situation must be included. Notice the circumstances surrounding the interaction which may weigh in on the emotional tenor.

Our awareness of the emotion behind the words we hear adds depth to our acknowledgment. *"I'm sensing a lot of sadness in your voice today."* We comfortably open one's heart to truthfulness and connectedness.

Recognizing Emotions

The best way to recognize emotions is to pay attention! People can mask feelings behind facial expressions, smiling when having a bad day, for example. Listen to the emotional *tone* or *emphasis* behind the words. Do they match the context of the situation? Interestingly, the words we hear are autobiographical. People can only express what is within their perceptual view, thinking, feeling, need, imagination, or desire.

Unfortunately, we often hear others state their desires indirectly. I hear someone ask me, *"Are you hungry?"* Who do you think is hungry? There is a good chance they are. We are asked, *"Are you happy?"* What we hear has a hint of self-interest buried within. We can answer or follow with a question (Part 2), *"What makes you ask that?"* to uncover the reason.

When we consider emotions, any confusion between <u>what we hear</u> and the <u>importance</u> of what is behind the words becomes more transparent. Charles asks me, *"Are you going to <u>THAT</u> meeting today?"* It sounds like he doesn't want to go to the meeting for some reason. I might respond, *"Sounds like you're concerned about the meeting."* This invites his truth if he cares to share.

We become better communicators when we are emotionally aware. When we *respond* with sensitivity to the emotional state of others, our words have a higher chance of getting through, leaving people with a willingness to reveal.

Finding the right word to describe an emotional state can be tricky. Our vocabulary to defend ourselves is often more forthcoming than our vocabulary to identify the emotion behind words.

If someone is *irritated,* their expression becomes terse, adding pressure to interpret what they mean. When we acknowledge the sentiment, *"I'm sensing irritation,"* we can create an opening to clarify meaning with a question, *"Do you care to share?"*

TIP: When emotions aren't apparent, we can bypass acknowledging and respond with a clarifying question. This is covered in Part 2.

Below is a list of forty-five common emotions found around emotional interactions. Increasing our emotional vocabulary will help us find the right word to acknowledge. *"I hear reluctance around Jim's decision."* We are not trying to solve their problem, just trying to create an opening to find out what they are perceiving. We can ask questions to understand, then talk it out if we choose. Trust is fostered because people feel we *"get"* them.

Common Emotions Found In Emotional Interactions		
Angry	Hurt	Reluctant
Annoyed	Horrified	Restless
Awkward	Heartbroken	Resentful
Bewildered	Irritated	Sad
Concerned	Isolated	Scared
Confused	Impatient	Stressed
Discouraged	Lonely	Troubled
Disgusted	Miserable	Uneasy
Embarrassed	Manipulated	Uncertain
Exasperated	Misunderstood	Unnerved
Fearful	Nervous	Unhappy
Furious	Offended	Unsure
Frustrated	Outraged	Vulnerable
Flustered	Overwhelmed	Worried
Humiliated	Pressured	Wronged

The stronger the emotion, the deeper the need (or hurt).

VALUES and NEEDS Behind the Words and Actions

*Values are like fingerprints. Nobody's are the same,
yet you leave them all over everything you do.* - Elvis Presley

Our values and needs are guiding principles behind what we *want*, *say*, and *do*. If I value something, I will protect it, thus central to consider when differences arise. Most disagreements result from a violation of our values or needs to which we are emotionally attached.

> **TIP:** Values and needs are universal and apply across cultures and generations.

Review the list of forty-five values and needs. On a piece of paper, prioritize the top ten most instrumental in shaping your life. There are hundreds of values and needs. Include any not listed.

Common Values and Needs

Achievement	Fairness	Personal Growth
Adventure	Flexibility	Privacy
Ambition	Freedom	Punctuality
Closeness	Frugality/Economy	Recognition
Calmness	Genuineness	Reliability
Commitment	Gratitude	Respect/Dignity
Competence	Harmony	Routine
Comfort	Honesty	Safety/Security
Competition	Hygiene	Spirituality
Conformity	Independence	Stability
Cooperation	Intimacy	Structure
Curiosity	Integrity	Support
Dependability	Kindness	Teamwork
Directness	Loyalty	Trustworthiness
Equality	Order	Variety

The **definition** and **importance** we place on each value or need vary from person to person. To illustrate, we may both want *intimacy* yet differ in how we define it, and how it is best supported.

How we express the same value differs from person to person. We both want *respect*, yet our definitions and validations can vary. We can *mitigate* many arguments ahead of time by clearly defining, discussing, understanding, (and accepting) contrasting values and needs. (See Appendix 1 on page 102 for a deeper dive into this topic.)

Our most satisfying interactions are with people who have similar values, interests, and needs. We may have difficulty with those whose values and needs conflict with our own. For example, if *routine* is comfortable to me and *variety* is needed by you, a conversation on how the two can co-exist is wise. *Routine* and *variety* can *both* be honored when accepted and discussed maturely.

Gretchen and Rob debate sleeping with the window open or closed. Both are adamant about their preference. Each is locked in either/or thinking—a mutually exclusive quandary when two things cannot happen simultaneously. If they continue to argue at the <u>Want</u> level, an obvious solution may be to compromise. Monday, Wednesday, and Friday, the window stays open all night. Tuesday, Thursday, and Saturday, the window remains closed. On Sunday, they flip a coin to decide. Both sacrifice something to get what they want. Not always satisfying, yet both yield for the sake of agreement.

On the other hand, if they go to the <u>Value</u> level, both can win without sacrifice. Instead of defending our position at the <u>Want</u> level, stop to find out <u>why</u> each wants the window open or closed. A real need is seeking satisfaction in both. What values are at stake? Bottom line: Rob wants to sleep in comfort, and Gretchen wants to feel safe and secure. Trying to convince Gretchen that she is safe communicates that Rob is not listening. Go further. They both agree they are entitled to a safe and comfortable night's sleep. The question becomes: What possible solutions are available to us to satisfy our definition of both comfort and security? This question directs our thinking to a new set of possibilities beyond the open or closed window option.

Such as: an alarm system, fan, a dog, bars in the window, a dowel in the window frame, separate bedrooms, etc. The brainstorming session redirects thinking toward solutions supporting the real reasons (Values) instead of arguing over an open or closed window (Wants). Now, each possible solution that satisfies both comfort and security can be discussed and narrowed down. Because they are saving money for a vacation, they agree on a dowel in the window frame that will open only so far, allowing fresh air to circulate to satisfy both their values and needs and concerns. Problem solved. When we go to the Value and Need level, we can let compromise be the last solution instead of the first.

Which Value or Need is at Stake

How do we know which value is at stake? People usually tell us what they value indirectly. Sometimes it is evident; other times, it is not. Regrettably, we hear people's values or needs most clearly behind complaints, criticisms, and blames.

Our associate says, for example, *"I want time to work alone, but you always interrupt me to have meetings throughout the day."* Instead of defending, we acknowledge, *"Working <u>without interruption</u> sounds important to you."* They respond, *"Yes!"* We will not solve the problem with our acknowledgment. We open the door to a more meaningful conversation by clarifying, *"How can we satisfy both working alone without interruption and still meet-up when needed?"* **We center the discussion on how their need of working alone can also satisfy my need to meet.** Unforeseen solutions emerge. When we first Acknowledge (A), then Clarify (C) intentions, we make it easier to Talk (T) without judgments, blame, or jumping to conclusions. Problem-solving can be more conversational and less stressful.

> **TIP:** What is the difference between a **Want** and a **Need**? A *want* is built on a desire, where a *need* is built on a more profound necessity or value. For example, I may want new tires for my car. I need new tires when they are flat or worn out and make driving unsafe.

Listed below are examples of possible values or needs hidden within a complaint or a request. Remember, our definition of each value or need is critical in coming up with a satisfying solution that works for *both*.

Complaint, Criticism, or Wants	Possible Value/Need at Play
"She invades my space all the time. I'm suffocating."	Privacy/Independence/Freedom vs. Closeness/Intimacy
"You change your mind so much, and I'm confused."	Variety/Flexibility vs. Safety/Routine/Trust
"I want to go out together once in a while, and you only want to stay home."	Closeness/Adventure/Fairness vs. Comfort/Routine/Privacy
"You are always late! How can I count on you?"	Variety vs. Stability/Respect
"I deserve that promotion! '	Recognition/Fairness/Respect

Once we become familiar with the vocabulary of emotions and values, we can listen to people through more skillful ears. *Complaints, criticisms, requests, desires,* and *wants* invite our curiosity instead of defensiveness.

We may find it harder to argue with someone wanting more *stability, closeness,* or *respect*. **What that looks like and how that happens is what we discuss.** We move away from either/or thinking into a place that opens more plausible solutions we wouldn't have otherwise seen. There is usually more than one way to satisfy a specific value or need.

However, there is one major limitation we may encounter—a fixed position. *"This is the way I want it, period!"* or *"We only do it this way around here."* We can hear the emotion behind their words. When we are unwilling to be flexible, we negate alternative solutions that will satisfy everyone's interests and needs.

We get a glimpse into people's inner world by how they respond to us.

What is Acknowledgment

We cannot motivate people,
only create an environment where people motivate themselves.

Acknowledgment Defined

Acknowledgment is an affirming and validating response to someone's comment, proposal, request, efforts, or opinion, whether we agree, disagree, or want to express understanding because we care.

Words such as *affirm, recognize, validate,* and *understand* are used synonymously. Acknowledgment is a skillful way of saying: *"I hear you," "I recognize you,"* or *"You're important."* The simplest and most basic form of acknowledgment is a *"Thanks"* or *"I'm sorry"* or *"Good job."* We can acknowledge others anytime for nearly anything.

The most skillful use of acknowledgment is when we *disagree.* It asks us to set aside our pride (and righteousness) long enough to *create* a receptive mood for civil discourse to follow. In other words, we hold back any emotionally charged reactions. Self-restraint works to our advantage by giving us time to *hear* and *respond* appropriately. If emotions escalate and words get too personal, it is best to pause and excuse ourselves until tempers cool. Talk is often defensive when strong emotions are present.

Acknowledging recognizes people's right to their truth, experience, opinion, or perspective. Deep down, people want to be accepted for who they are without judgment.

Key Benefits of Acknowledging

When I acknowledge, I can:

- Calm escalating emotions.
- Make my decision to engage or not to engage clear.
- Let someone know they were heard, noticed, or appreciated.
- Create a seamless opening to ask questions to clarify.
- Express understanding for someone's challenging experience.
- End a conversation tactfully.

We know our acknowledgment was accepted when we get a *"Yes!"*, *"Thank you,"* an affirming *nod*, or a *calm* reaction. If our disclosure is off the mark, we can follow with, *"Help me understand. What are you experiencing?"* People become willing to answer questions and talk when they feel heard. We have created a suitable condition to move a delicate conversation forward or end it gracefully. Talk is not conducive when emotions are highly charged.

Acknowledgment is the *first skill* in the A.C.T. Way to respond to everyday communication. We create the right atmosphere to clarify, talk, resolve, or conclude. More willing ears occur after Acknowledging (A), especially when we hear passionate comments from others. *"I hear this is important to you."* Our brief statement verifies we heard without agreement, consent, judgment, or endorsement of their view. We then ask questions to Clarify (C) what we're hearing, then Talk (T) to share our views.

Erin in H.R. is assigned to deliver bad news to Ryan. He is not getting the promotion. Erin calls Ryan into her office, where she shares the decision. Ryan responds, "But I deserve that promotion!" Erin adds, "We've made our decision. Sorry, you're not getting it this time around." Ryan is demoralized.

Here is how the conversation might go using A.C.T. Acknowledge (A) the real need why Ryan wants the promotion. "Ryan, I hear more recognition is important to you. Is that correct?" Ryan replies, "Yes!" Erin moves to Clarifying (C) with questions. "Let us explore alternatives. Can I ask you some questions?" Ryan nods, okay. "What else could we do to bring you more recognition?" Ryan lists several things he would like changed in the department. Erin and Ryan then Talk (T) over the options, agreeing on several. One discussion is regarding what Ryan can do to get a promotion and mapping out the strategy. Both win. Despite Ryan not getting exactly what he wanted, he did get other things to satisfy his need for recognition.

TIP: If Ryan responds *"No"* to *"I hear more recognition is important to you,"* follow with, *"Then what is important?"* If he insists, *"The promotion."* Ask questions to discover the Value or Need behind his response until *"why it's important"* is clear. (Refer to Part 2, page 43 on Clarify for more detail.)

It is far easier to support someone in getting what they want, when getting what and why they want it is clear.

Chapter   **3**

The Power of Acknowledgment

When one will not, two cannot argue.

Have you ever encountered someone who pushes your buttons, resulting in an argument you did not invite? We all have. My friend, William, has a reputation for being a contrarian. He will ask a question, listen, then respond with an opposing view inciting debate that sometimes gets heated. Finally, after forty years of friendship and falling into his trap time after time, I decided to change my response. While watching a game together one afternoon, he asked a question to which I responded. As usual, he shared the opposite viewpoint. Instead of defending my differing perspective, I said, *"That's another way to look at it."* A miracle happened! Like a period at the end of a sentence, he had nothing else to add. During the second half of the game, he asked another question. I responded, he responded, and I followed with, *"That too is another way to look at it."* Nowhere to go, he went silent.

It was another three weeks before William tried his usual tactic, which again I followed with, *"That sure is another way to look at it."* The word among our friends was that he miraculously stopped playing the contrarian game. William realized that this tactic no longer worked for him. He changed on his own accord. I had changed too, ending a decade's long folly, which I found irritating at times. I realized how I *respond* matters.

Beyond friendly banter, why set ourselves up for a useless debate when we can acknowledge and put their comment to rest? Once we engage in a disagreement, our emotions heighten, our listening fades, our thinking narrows, and our choices shrink.

HOW to Acknowledge

I never saw an instance of one of two disputants convincing the other by argument. - Thomas Jefferson

Acknowledgment is not summarizing or agreeing per se. **It is recognizing and validating the experience <u>the other person</u> is having.** If I hear something and beg to differ, instead of challenging or attempting to resolve it right away, acknowledge first.

Why does this work? We all want to be heard without confrontation, whether right or wrong. We respect the right to an opinion. Just because my opinion differs does not make me wrong.

When it is essential to share my side, acknowledge their side first. This helps us move the conversation to a place where they are apt to listen. If my emotional meter begins to rise, and I want to avoid anger, I will postpone the discussion for another time. I walk away if words have become too personal. Temper is what gets us into an argument. Pride is what keeps us there.

WHEN to Acknowledge

*At the close of our monthly meetings, we share suggestions on improving the department's efficiency. During one session, Jeff goes on and on about a money-saving idea for our team. Since he is new, short on experience, and eager to please, I could easily interrupt and poke holes in his proposal in front of the group. I could embarrass Jeff and feel superior at the cost of maybe losing a future ally. Instead, **when he finished**, I acknowledged him by saying, "I sense your excitement and enthusiasm about your proposal, Jeff." He responded with an emphatic "Yes!" I followed with Test Questions (Ch 8) that inspired a thought-provoking discussion to improve his idea. Everyone wins. Acknowledging (**A**) and Clarifying (**C**) paved the way to make Talk (**T**) more productive without a need to make someone wrong. We create the right environment <u>first</u> for an exchange to occur, <u>especially</u> when emotions are present.*

Three Opportunities to Acknowledge

There are three common opportunities to acknowledge: **I agree** or **genuinely care** about you, **I disagree** with you, or **I agree in part**. Let us review examples of the language to use for each opportunity.

1 Acknowledge When I Agree or Genuinely Care

If we agree with what we hear, a courteous reply of: *"I like that idea"* or *"Sounds good"* or *"That will work"* will suffice. This confirms we're on the same page and verifies what we heard. If we choose to explore their thoughts in more detail, we can clarify by asking the right kind of questions (Part 2), then talk through any variations (Part 3). My acknowledgment will serve to end the discussion as well.

When we genuinely care, we are more generous with our time and ears. Listening becomes more patient and compassionate with our spouse, children, partner, friend, or close associates. If my best friend's father passes away, I say, *"I'm so sorry, Peter. I know how close you were to your dad. I'm there for you, my friend."* My acknowledgment demonstrates I care and validates the importance of our relationship.

Over dinner, my son Andrew shared how his 1st-grade teacher got mad in front of the class. I could hear fear in Andrew's voice. I acknowledge, "That must have been scary for you." "Yes," he replied. Now, I can ask a question, and my son will feel safe to respond knowing I understand.

Sometimes *silence* is the best acknowledgment. Not everything requires a response. People may not welcome my advice on how to fix their problem, unless they have asked. It is best to say nothing and listen. In other emotional situations, a silent nod or a hug, if appropriate, may serve. Silence is a response that can communicate more than words.

Being respectful to people we dislike is a skill.

Martha is a customer service representative for a local utility company. I ask her to explain a typical day to me. She says, *"I handle complaints all day long. When the phone rings, I pick up and hear, 'My power is off, and I paid my bill! Why don't you people do your job!' I sense their payment was not received, but first, I deal with the emotion (Strong emotion equals compromised listening). If I told them we didn't receive their payment, emotions could quickly escalate. Instead, I acknowledge their experience: 'I hear your frustration, and you want your power turned back on ASAP.' 'YES!' they respond. 'Let's see what happened.' If their emotions calm down, I can help get them what they want. If they are still terse and emotional, I set a boundary and respond with, 'I want to help you resolve this, though I need for us to talk calmly. Are you willing to do that?' If they agree, I continue to negotiate ways to solve their problem. If they are still too emotional, I ask that they call back when we can talk more calmly. I set limits on what I will and what I will not tolerate helping them get what they want. If the other person is not ready to respect this process, I postpone until they are."*

A little chaos is part of any disagreement. Though, when the arrow of anger becomes personally directed, the tone takes a turn. Keeping our emotions intact is extremely difficult when the attack is personal. Advancing disagreement into personal attacks drives away fruitful discussion and undermines resolution. Our aggravation makes it impossible to hear the other person's experience, distorting our perspective. Have you ever resolved a problem through an arguing match? It rarely happens.

Ways to Avoid an Argument

Never argue with a fool, they'll drag you down to their level, then beat you with their experience. - Mark Twain

<table>
<tr><td>A)</td><td>Acknowledge their experience after we hear it. We may not like what we hear, yet people are entitled to their opinion. "I hear this is important to you. Would you like to talk about it?" As long as it doesn't turn into a personal attack after acknowledging, I follow with questions for clarification and then talk. We dramatically increase our chance to turn their opinion into a calm dialogue.</td></tr>
<tr><td>B)</td><td>Set a Boundary or Limit before emotions start to thunder into an acrimonious debate, denying us from getting what we want. State my experience first. "I'm getting uncomfortable with the tone of this conversation and need time to think this through." Or, "I'm getting upset and prefer to talk when I'm calm." We then agree to a future discussion with relaxed emotions if a resolution is needed. If I hear, "We're going to talk right now!", I recognize their emotions are too high to have a cordial conversation and walk away by saying, "I prefer to talk later."</td></tr>
<tr><td>C)</td><td>Listen to that which we disagree. When words become personal, our instinct goes on high alert, yet we <u>refrain</u> from saying things we may later regret. We decide we're not in a position to challenge this person by getting up to leave. The cost would be too great. We stand mute, yielding to the authority. We are in a dreadful and uncomfortable position. Life is full of unreasonable people who invalidate us. We realize people are who they are. We later rethink the value of this relationship or situation in our life and decide accordingly.</td></tr>
</table>

Devon tells me he uses a nonverbal signal to avoid an argument before it escalates. *"After numerous all-out arguments at work, Sally and I have agreed that when one gets upset during a discussion, either can use a <u>time-out hand gesture</u>. Postponing a heated conversation gives us the distance to calm down and think more clearly. Also, to ensure fairness during our discussions, we <u>raise a hand</u> instead of verbally interrupting when one goes on and on. Our work relationship has become far more collaborative as a result."*

I don't have to attend every argument I'm invited to. - W.C. Fields

As my mentor would often say, *"Much of what we hear are half-truths. When we hear a half-truth, look for the other half!"* Instead of interrupting to share our half, <u>acknowledge their half first</u> by agreeing in part. Not every criticism, complaint, or judgment flying our direction deserves a response or is a reason to get defensive about. I only hear half the truth. *Their truth!* Agree in part and move on until the time is right.

Outright consenting when we disagree is insincere and may come back to haunt us. Agreeing in part verifies we heard one side (theirs) until we have time to discuss the other side (ours).

A few years ago I received an email from an orthopedic surgeon who took my class because the hospital required him to improve his communication skills. The surgical nurses he worked with complained of his gruff demeanor. He wrote, *"Learning to acknowledge and ask questions changed my life. Now, when a nurse brings me a complaint, instead of arguing to defend myself, I respond sincerely with: You may be right. If the issue is ongoing or necessary, I will ask: Would you like to talk about this later? It bypasses resolving now and usually calms the emotions, saving me time when I'm too busy to talk."*

How might we respond to various criticisms by agreeing in part? We agree in part by using the **key word** in their comment:

They Say	I Agree in Part
"You're <u>too sensitive</u>."	*"Yes, I am sensitive. Thank you."*
"You're <u>disrespectful</u>."	*"Yes, I can be disrespectful at times."*
"You're always <u>critical</u>."	*"You're right, I can be critical at times."*
"You never <u>listen</u>."	*"You're right, I could listen better."*
"You're always <u>selfish</u>."	*"You're right, I can be selfish at times."*

"You are an <u>idiot</u>!"	*"You're right, I can be foolish at times."*
"<u>You're nuts</u> thinking that way"	*"That's one way to look at it."*

Annie tells me a story about Erica, an astute, articulate associate who loves to give people unsolicited advice. Annie explains, *"We hear a lot of 'you should' prefacing her suggestions. Many have told her to mind her own business, yet she continues. Instead of disagreeing with her advice and getting into a rebuttal, I go with it by saying in a friendly tone: 'Thank you, Erica' or 'I'll think about that' or 'Thanks for your insight. I'm busy right now.' Acknowledging her unsolicited help will perhaps stop her from bothering me in the future. My respectful approach may lead her toward more receptive targets that satisfy her need to give advice or draw debate."*

Agreeing in part does not solve the problem, but it usually ends the distraction. There is no need to be flippant. Be sincere. If we choose to discuss it at a later date, we conclude with a question. *"Do you want to talk about this later?"* and pick a convenient time.

Words to Use for an Acknowledgment

Below are examples of words to begin a statement of acknowledgment:

"That must be_____________ to you."

"That sounds _____________ for you."

"I'm hearing that must be ___________."

"I hear the ___________ in your voice."

"I can only imagine how___________ that is for you."

"I'm sensing ___________ around such and such."

Fill in the blank with a word that best captures <u>*their*</u> experience, (challenging, difficult, frustrating etc). We can confirm by asking, *"Is that right?"* If they say, *"No,"* follow with, *"Help me understand. What are you experiencing?"* This creates a suitable condition to ask questions and talk.

How <u>Not</u> to Acknowledge

Anger is one letter short of DANGER. - Eleanor Roosevelt

Acknowledging has nothing to do with fixing, judging, assessing, giving advice, parroting, or criticizing. It is our starting point to neutralize or calm the emotion (if present) behind the comment we hear. The following examples compare ways *not to* and ways *to* acknowledge.

Judges their experience	Acknowledges their experience
"You shouldn't be so hard on yourself."	*"That must be <u>hard</u> on you."*
"You should talk to a therapist."	*"It sounds <u>confusing</u> for you."*
"You should break-up with them."	*"I'm hearing they're <u>challenging</u> to you."*
"You are being way too sensitive."	*"That sounds <u>uncomfortable</u> for you."*
"Can't you listen better."	*"I'm hearing that's <u>unclear</u> to you."*
"Oh, I know how you feel."	*"I'm sensing <u>sadness</u> in your voice."*

Which statements are more likely to get a *"Yes"* or *"Thank you"* reply? A judgment or assessment <u>*is not*</u> an acknowledgment. We find the right word to acknowledge through noting the *other* person's experience.

A colleague approaches me after work on a Friday complaining about having the worst week of his life. I could respond, "Get over it. Life is tough!" However, advising or dismissing does not acknowledge. People appreciate feeling heard when they need to vent. It is more helpful for me to say, "I'm sorry you are having such a stressful week." It cost me little, yet yields tremendous goodwill with the options to move on, ask questions, or talk it through.

A sensitive response supports the favor returned when we need a kind ear to listen.

Chapter 4

Acknowledge the Strength Built On a Weakness

People fall not from their weakness,
but from their strengths gone to excess. - Aeschylus

Bringing up our critical assessment of others in a conversation rarely gets us what we want. Our uninvited judgments only serve to turn people away. Continually reminding other's of their short-comings has a hidden cost over time; <u>it chips away at the heart of our relationship</u>. However, there are times when we may need to address a perceived weakness that may be causing a problem at work or home. This can be done in a positive way by determining and acknowledging the strength built on that weakness. Examples:

Perceived Weaknesses Mode of Expression	The Strength Behind that Weakness Shifting Perspective
Procrastinator	Patient/Cautious/Safety minded
Aggressive	Gets things done/Action oriented
Intense	Highly focused/Motivated
Know it all	Well-informed/Willing to share
Dominant Big Ego	Dynamic/Charismatic/Confident
Argumentative	Quick minded/Stands up for self
Indecisive	Sees many options/Thinks through
Stubborn	Strong conviction around the subject
Controlling	Has a vision/Knows what they want
Interrupting	Quick thinker/Important need to share
Micromanaging	Detail oriented/Cautious/Has a vision

Shifting Perspective

*Change the way you look at something
and the thing you look at changes.* - Wayne Dyer

Shifting perspective helps us find alternative words to address our concern. The weakness we experience is often an *overreaction* or *compensation* of their strength. This perspective can help us relate to people's troubling behaviors in a whole new light.

The words we choose to define our displeasure can help our effort to create a solution. If we aim to discuss a specific behavior and how it unproductively plays out, change the language from negative labels on what they do wrong to the strength behind that trait. **Acknowledge their power, not their weakness, and avoid a defensive response.** Below are examples of what that may sound like when we focus on a weakness versus acknowledge the strength:

Focus on Weakness	Acknowledge Strength
"You are a <u>know-it-all!</u>"	*"I'm hearing you are <u>well informed</u> on the issue."*
"You have a <u>big ego!</u>"	*"You're a <u>very dynamic</u> person."*
"You are so <u>stubborn.</u>"	*"I sense <u>strong convictions</u> on this project."*
"You're so <u>indecisive!</u>"	*"I get the feeling you <u>see many options</u>."*
"You're a <u>micromanager!</u>"	*"I sense you're <u>cautious</u> and <u>have a vision</u>."*
"Can't you stop <u>interrupting?</u>"	*"I hear something is <u>important to you</u>."*

There is a difference between calling someone *argumentative* versus *quick-minded*. One word sounds like criticism, while the other sounds like an asset. When we use affirming words, we make it easier for them to listen and feel safe opening up to us.

Acknowledging others' strengths helps us gain favorable attention upon what we say next. Here are some example:

Getting interrupted: *"I hear something is important to you. Would you hold that thought until I finish?"*

Sensing indecisiveness: *"I get the impression you see many options to the decision. Want to talk them through?"*

Procrastinating: *"I notice you are very patient and cautious with the project. What can we do to speed up the process?"*

Someone being stubborn: *"I sense a strong conviction on doing it this way. Are you open to help me understand?"*

This response moves the conversation into a more favorable realm making it easy for them to be open to discuss. (See Appendix 3, page 105 for additional examples.)

What can an enemy do when the opponent is cordial.

Getting Our Buttons Pushed

Some days it seems people are put on this earth for no other reason than to annoy me. - Kin Hubbard

Listening often takes a back seat when our buttons get pushed, activating our *fight-flight-freeze* instinct. When our pride and dignity feel challenged, a heated exchange or a collapsed discussion may be near.

By <u>arousing</u> our usual *reaction*, our hot buttons hold us hostage, adding uninvited drama into our lives. People get to know our buttons over time. Some people are very clever in using our weaknesses to get what they want. Unfortunately, a few even seek pleasure in seeing others hurt, upset, or uncomfortable. People's approaches and words say more *about them* than *about us*.

When *frustration grows*, our words can quickly become judgmental, turning what we mean to say into criticism. Note how each set of statements would yield an entirely different conversation.

What Frustration Expresses	What We Really Mean
"You're always late and keep me waiting!"	*I'd like for you to arrive on time.*
"You wear the same thing every day."	*I like variety in my clothing.*
"You screwed up on that project."	*I would do some things differently.*
"You always fight with Nicholas."	*I'd like you and Nicholas to get along.*
"You make a mess in the refrigerator."	*I prefer an organized refrigerator.*

Are our words meant to criticize or inspire change? There are better ways to state what we want. That's not to say constructive feedback isn't occasionally beneficial when respectfully applied.

Recognizing Our Buttons

I have more trouble with D.L Moody
than any other person I know. - D.L. Moody

Our interactions can be hurtful and intense at times, especially when our buttons get pushed unexpectedly. When that happens, it can bring out the worst in us. It is far easier to default into our instinct (with anger) than to respond consciously and skillfully in the moment. Of course, we can always retreat. Once emotions kick in, our ability to think clearly and listen is diminished.

Someone once quipped, *"I may have pushed your buttons, though I wasn't the one who installed them!"* If we blame others for pushing our buttons, we do not solve the problem. The ultimate struggle is within.

Notice if our <u>same button</u> gets pressed repeatedly. Reflect upon the situations where our buttons get pushed—with *whom*, what was *said* or *done* to test it. Take an honest look at *why* we are sensitive and where that sensitivity was born. Perhaps an awareness of these triggers can help give us some distance or detachment. Review which *values* are at stake (Page 16). Does my definition of my value place unrealistic limits and expectations on others?

Working on our buttons is a lifelong process. When we outgrow one, someone comes along to expose another. Life's invitation for growth is inevitable. We have a choice: a different reaction will bring us a different outcome.

The greatest conflicts are not between two people, but between one person and himself. - Garth Brooks

Rewards From Recognition

Expressing Appreciation

Kindness has its own reward.

Pointing out faults is counterproductive. We have a better way. We can extend an appreciation or a compliment, which will encourage or inspire. It is always beneficial to state our observation of what we *do appreciate* versus *don't like*. Praise works wonders for the sense of hearing. We make people feel good about themselves, and they respect us for noticing. Reinforce the behavior we want in others.

Bill told me that Jerry, a shop supervisor saved the company $10,000 with a simple yet effective idea. I asked Bill, the department manager, "Was a memo of appreciation written to Jerry?" "No," Bill responded. I followed, "Would that be helpful?" Bill immediately sat down at his computer and composed a brief letter of congratulations, thanking Jerry for what he did and explained why the company valued his ingenuity. He also cc'd H.R. and the company president. I watched Jerry read the delivered note noticing how he beamed in delight and then shared his excitement with his team. I turned to Bill and watched his face glow. Did the letter of recognition cost the manager anything but a few minutes? What message did that gesture send?

TIP: We express appreciation by noticing a <u>specific</u> strength, a characteristic, an effort for something someone did or said, and why it's of merit. It costs us nothing, yet we disclose, *"I notice you, and you're valued."* Everyone wants to be appreciated and recognized. There is a lot of joy in celebrating the success of others.

Insincere Compliments

It is possible to experience a *downside* to overusing compliments. For example, if I receive too many compliments from Skyler, I might wonder, *"What does he want from me?"* We may feel good because someone took notice yet question their motive when overdone.

If we sense an insincere compliment, ask a question to clarify. *"Thank you! What makes that important to you?"* Since we usually hear *what* they liked, we have a right to understand *why* that was important to them. It won't be long before you stop hearing *insincere* or *empty* compliments.

Giving a Sincere Compliment

Be specific about the incident you're praising. When we are clear-cut about the *time* and *place* it happened and *why* it was of value to us, we make the compliment genuine. The receiver's mind validates sincerity by recalling the incident and its effects. We get a smile, thanks, and a bright attitude in return!

A Sincere Compliment Includes:

WHAT specific thing did I notice and WHEN (Action).
WHY that's important to me or others (Effect).

"Lauren, I appreciate your questions at yesterday's sales meeting,
(What+When)
because it spurred a meaningful discussion among the staff." (Why)

When we *sparingly* and *sincerely* acknowledge with a compliment, we support people's dignity and find they usually remember and reciprocate.

I went to the local cable company store to make a change to my account. Zoe was the young woman who helped me. While standing between two other service representatives helping customers, Zoe focused her attention on my needs. Another representative walked up and interrupted to ask Zoe a question. She smiled at me, turned to answer, and then turned back to me. A few moments later, the representative helping a customer to her right turned and interrupted us to ask a question of her. She replied and turned back to me with an apologetic smile. We continued. A few minutes later, the representative to her left interrupted to ask a question. At this point, it would be easy for me to get frustrated with all the distractions. Instead, I looked at an exasperated Zoe. I said, "You seem very organized and knowledgeable, Zoe (The What), because your associates rely on your expertise for answers to their questions." (The Why) She stopped, looked at me, and said, "Thank you so much for noticing that." We finished our business without further delay, and she unexpectedly waived the $50 service fee and smiled. People will usually go out of their way to help those they like.

Apology

If we admit we're wrong when we are wrong, we are right.

When we argue who is right or wrong, we pit our pride and ego against theirs, often escalating the situation without resolution. Do we want to admit we're wrong when we feel we are right? Of course not! Our sincerity is in question if we appease for the sake of peace. *"Alright, I'm sorry."* An insincere and empty apology undermines trust and confidence.

When We Are Wrong

If we are wrong, admit it quickly and <u>unconditionally</u>. We ultimately feel better about ourselves by taking responsibility for our actions or part. Make our apology genuine and sincere by including the reason(s) why we're sorry (What +Why). An apology can be given at any time, either written or spoken.

Examples of how that might sound:

"You were right. There was a better way for me to handle the situation."

*"I didn't realize I was doing that;
it was not my intention to harm. I'm sorry."*

*"Thank you for bringing this to my attention.
I was wrong for handling it that way."*

*"I was having a terrible day,
and I'm sorry for taking it out on you. I apologize."*

When We Are Right

What if we are right? If the issue persists, we extend an *acknowledgment*. Instead of falsely admitting we're wrong, acknowledge *their* experience or regret for the harm done to them through the incident in question. This allows both of us to save face. This approach is influential at all levels of power or authority. A news story to illustrate:

Six weeks into a standoff over a collision between an American intelligence aircraft and a Chinese fighter jet over the China Sea in 2001, China wanted the United States to apologize. The crash caused the death of a PRC pilot, and the American plane had to make an emergency landing on the island of Hainan in China. The Chinese authorities detained the twenty-four crew members until the United States government delivered a statement regarding the incident. China wanted an admission of wrongdoing which the United States refused.

There was no resolution with both the cause of the collision and the assignment of blame in dispute. The administration did not want to admit fault. Instead, followed by a letter to Chinese diplomats, George W. Bush went on TV to say, "The United States is very sorry for the death of the Chinese pilot, Wang Wei, and the pain caused to his family. We are also very sorry the aircraft entered China's airspace and landed not having verbal clearance."

Without admitting guilt, the United States <u>acknowledged</u> regret for the incident. The pilots were quickly released. We apologized by _validating_ their experience without admitting fault. Both saved face.

We usually contribute *something* to a dispute. Pride may cause difficulty exacting our part. Reflecting on our contribution goes a long way towards extending and receiving an apology in return. If the other person apologizes, we best take responsibility for how we responded to the incident. *"Thanks for saying that. I could have reacted in a better way as well."* Apologizing for our part builds openness and trust.

The best chance we have getting past people's defenses is to be honest, authentic, and vulnerable when it's most difficult. We allow others to experience our humanness. The *perceived* risk may be high, yet the outcome often makes up for our concerns. There are times we lose our temper, press too forcefully, or push beyond others' boundaries. It's okay to say we're sorry. We demonstrate emotional maturity.

A clear conscience laughs at false accusations.

√ When people speak, there is far more to what they say than what we hear. When we listen _carefully_, we tune in to the speaker's interests, emotions, values, and needs behind their words.

√ When we consider emotions, any confusion between _what we hear_ and the _importance_ becomes more transparent.

√ Our Values or Needs are guiding _principles_ behind what we _want_, _say_, and _do_. How we express the same value differs from person to person. We both want _respect_, yet our definitions and validations may vary.

√ Most disagreements result from a violation of our values or needs to which we are emotionally attached.

√ Acknowledgment is an affirming and validating response to someone's comment, proposal, request, efforts, or opinion, whether we agree, disagree, or want to express understanding because we care.

√ Acknowledgment is not summarizing or agreeing per se. We respond by validating the experience the other person is having. Instead of challenging or attempting to resolve a difference of opinion right away, acknowledge first to create the condition to talk.

√ Acknowledging what we hear has _nothing_ to do with fixing, judging, assessing, giving advice, parroting, or criticizing. It is our _starting_ point to _neutralize_ or _calm_ the emotion (if present) behind the comment we hear. Talk is not conducive when emotions are highly charged.

√ Continually reminding others of their shortcomings has a hidden cost over time; it chips away at the heart of our relationship.

When we understand the other person's viewpoint or story,
and they understand ours, then we can sit down
and talk out our differences.

PART TWO

Clarify

The A.C.T. Way to Respond to Everyday Communication Without Argument

Acknowledge   **Clarify**   **Talk**

Emotional →→→ Conversational

Emotional Zone	**Discovery Zone**	**Discussion Zone**
Calm emotions by validating their experience to let them know they were heard.	Ask the right question to clarify their view before sharing ours.	

Strong emotions compromise the ability to reason and listen.

Asking the Right Question

There are many angles to the truth. - G.K. Chesterton

In our world of dualistic thinking (*yes/no, up/down, hot/cold, left/right, either/or*), the opposition between viewpoints is natural. No one viewpoint has a monopoly on reality. Consensus is not necessarily the truth.

Communication has *at least* two sides—ours and theirs. We live life invested in our *perspective*, sustained by our values, needs, relationships, and personal histories. The *easiest* way to clarify another's point of view is by asking the right kinds of questions.

My mentor said, *"What people say is like a piece of Swiss cheese. Fill in the holes, and you'll get a clearer picture."* We can fill in what we hear with assumptions, judgments, and interruptions **or** be curious and seek clarification and understanding.

When we ask the right *kind* of question at the right *time*, we invite someone to expand upon their perspective. Thus, it allows us to *adjust* our response to more accurate information, side-stepping assumptions. Bring transparency and clarity to ideas, requests, deceits, complaints, or proposals by asking questions.

Three high school boys skip first period to go out to breakfast. Upon arriving back to school, they run into their teacher. "Sorry about missing first hour, Ms. Fletcher. We got a flat tire on the way to school." Ms. Fletcher lets them know, "Boys, you missed a pop quiz. I'm willing to give you credit if you take a moment to complete it before your next class starts. Follow me and take a seat apart from one another." The boys sit down and wait for instructions.

She then tells them, "Take out a pen and a piece of paper and answer the following question: Which tire was flat?"

Often things are left unsaid or unclear when people communicate. Sometimes the facts are embellished or understated. Asking questions protects us from drawing the wrong conclusions. Clarity lies a few questions away.

Our questions prompt the recipient to think and illuminate their thoughts and feelings around the subject they're expressing. Before we share our opinion, start by asking a question. We listen to get an accurate picture to adjust our message for more accommodating ears.

Three Types of Questions

There are many types of questions. We will focus on three kinds that clarify what people *say, mean,* and *do* in everyday communication. They are: Follow-up questions, Test questions, and Resolving questions.

1 *After* we hear a request, an opinion, proposal, or view, we ask a <u>Follow-up question</u> to protect us from being misled or from jumping to conclusions.

2 A <u>Test question</u> is asked *before* and/or *after* to measure an idea's thinking or validity.

3 Finally, a <u>Resolving question</u> invites a discussion around a lingering issue we want to be resolved. Resolving questions are used to find a solution to a new or an ongoing problem.

All three types help us bridge the gap between what someone says or does and what they mean. Thus, we verify the importance, truth, and motivation of their thoughts and actions.

Using the right questions with friends, family, clients, or colleagues can free us of assumptions and help us make decisions based on more accurate information. When we ask a question, people include information they wouldn't have otherwise.

Why We Don't Ask Questions

Without the right question, the truth is often hidden.

What prevents us from asking questions? Could it be we fear we will ask the wrong question, look stupid, weak, or unsure in front of others? Do we find it more comforting to silently make assumptions about what others mean than to clarify and gain certainty? Do we figure it takes too much time, or think we already know the answer? We live in a talk and tell culture and want to give the impression we are confident and knowledgeable.

One of the most common complaints I hear others tell me after an interview, a first date, or a work meeting is, *"I wish they had asked me more questions."* Asking questions is a sign of strength and intelligence, leading to understanding and connectedness. We are naturally receptive to an appropriate question and want to share our ideas and feel heard. The first step to becoming a better questioner (and listener) is to get in the habit of asking the right question at the right time.

Curiosity has its own reason for existing. - Albert Einstein

Chapter 7

Follow-up Questions

The person asking questions usually leads the conversation.

Understanding the Words We Hear

Ask follow-up questions **after** someone says something, inviting an elaboration about what they meant. Like a magnifying glass, we see their meaning more clearly.

We can ask questions around six subjects: The *who, where, when, what, why,* and *how.* Each question divulges a specific piece of the bigger picture.

Who, where, and *when* questions are **fact-gathering**, providing us answers to the person, place, or time. We hear the response as a brief phrase or a one-word answer. Fact-gathering questions fill in *specific details* of an idea, plan, or agreement. Examples:

WHO	The Person	*"Who will be there?"*
WHERE	The Place	*"Where is it located?"*
WHEN	The Time	*"When will it be done?"*

Fact-gathering questions are best used **at the end** of a discussion unless these are the only answers we seek. When we ask, they tend to *conclude* a thought, not continue one.

On the other hand, *what, why,* and *how* questions are noted for their **perception-gathering** quality, clarifying one's perspective, reasoning, actions, opinions, and requests. We bring forth a deeper meaning and understanding. When asked, they tend to *open* and *continue* a thought.

<table>
<tr><td>**WHAT**</td><td>The Perspective</td><td>*"What makes you say that?"*</td></tr>
<tr><td>**WHY**</td><td>The Reason</td><td>*"Why is that so?"*</td></tr>
<tr><td>**HOW**</td><td>The Action/Steps</td><td>*"How does that happen?"*</td></tr>
</table>

When we ask a follow-up question *after* someone's comment, we open a smooth and natural transition to clarify what we heard: *"I think you're being pessimistic."* I respond, *"What makes you say that, Joe?"* We draw out a distinct and specific meaning or definition behind what was said.

> **TIP:** Many disagreements occur from misunderstandings and differences in perspective. Because we perceive things differently, it does not make us wrong. Most arguments happen when we react before clarifying.

The Challenging WHY Question

The tongue reflects what the mind thinks.

Starting with a *Why* question, we can appear aggressive, pressuring others to explain themselves. Why questions quickly put people on the spot. *"Why did you do that?"* or *"Why do you always think like that?"* or *"Why didn't you do it like Alice does?"* We fuel defensiveness. Do we always know why we do things? Instead, convert a *why* into a *what* question and make the implication vanish:

"<u>Why</u> did you do that?" Convert into *"<u>What</u> inspired your decision?"*

"<u>Why</u> are you so critical? Convert into *"<u>What</u> makes that important?"*

"<u>Why</u> are you always saying that?" Convert into *"<u>What</u> makes you say that?"*

Notice how the tone shifts when converting a *why* into a *what* question, making it more inviting to answer.

Does that mean all *why* questions are confrontational? Of course not. *Why* questions as a <u>follow-up</u> to someone's request or opinion can be valuable. For example: *"Why is that?"* or *"Why do you think that is?"* When responding to a risky request or proposal, ask: *"Why would I agree to that?"* Receive an insult or attack on our character, we might say: *"Why would you say something like that to me?"*

Where to Find the Next Question

Why assume when we can ask?

Suppose their answer still left us with questions. Follow up with another question. Where do we find the next question? Base our next question on their ***previous response***. Draw upon a ***keyword(s)*** from their answer to invite more detail. A co-worker says, *"Andrew is impossible to work with!"* Follow with, *"How do you mean?"* They respond, *"He is always so difficult."* Follow with the keyword, *"Difficult how?"* **Any term used to respond is open and reasonable territory for a follow-up question** when seeking further clarification. Question(s) narrows meaning into more specific and definable terms. Continue or stop asking at any point when satisfied. The other person feels heard.

Encountering reluctance to a follow-up question, say, *"I just want to understand more clearly."* Remember, others want to be understood and usually accommodate when sincere.

> **TIP:** Ever get too wordy of a response? Intervene with, *"That's a lot. What is most important for me to remember?"* Ever listen to a story go on and on? Ask, *"What finally happened?"* Excuse ourselves if they continue to be uncomfortably long-winded. People who take their time take ours. Close with, *"Perhaps we can pick this up at another time."*

Twenty-one Follow-up Questions

Below is a list of twenty-one follow-up questions. The questions are not in any particular order. Our follow-up questions are <u>neutral</u>. There is nothing *suggestive, leading, indirect,* or *assumptive* built into the question when asked. Thus, exclude any influence upon the person's answer. A little practice will help fine-tune the next question(s) to ask. (See Appendix 2 for additional questions. Page 103.)

Examples of Follow-up Questions

"How do you mean?"
"What makes you say that?"
"What led to that conclusion?"
"Why is that?"
"What does that look like to you?"
"How do you define...?"
"How do you see the situation."
"Why do you think that is so?"
"How do you wish it was?"
"How would you like to see it fixed?"
"How do we move forward?"
"What makes that important to you?"
"Is that realistic?"
"How so?"
"And?"
"Because?"
"For example?"
"Which means?"
"Then what?"
"In what way?"
"Such as?"

TIP: The question, *"How do you mean?"* may be questionable grammar, yet softens the sometimes confronting *"What do you mean?"* question.

Clarifying Further

A conversation is a dialogue, not a monologue. - Truman Capote

Occasionally, we find someone who does not feel safe sharing the real reason(s) in their initial response. Be patient and allow the ease of follow-up questions to gain further clarification. By favoring *what* and *how* questions, we uncover the deeper reasons behind a response. A more complete picture is usually three to five questions away. The goal is to move a general response into specifics or substantive facts. Follow-up questions make this natural, giving the feeling of a conversation instead of an interrogation.

Others want to be understood and welcome a nonjudgmental inquiry. Sensitivity on *how far* to follow-up becomes apparent with practice. Here is an example of how a conversation might sound between a mother and son:

Mom asks her son after dinner: *"Have you finished your homework?"*
Son: *"I don't want to."*
> (Calmly offset defiance with a follow-up question.)

Mom: *"What makes you say that, Son?"*
Son: *"I don't like it?"*
> (Base the next question on a keyword used to respond.)

Mom: *"What don't you like about it."*
Son: *"It's stupid!"*
> (Again, base the following question on the keyword.)

Mom: *"Stupid how?"*
Son: *"The problems are too hard."*
> (Ah, finally the fact or truth, and real reason.)

Mom: *"Shall we work on them together?"*
Son: *"Okay."*
> (Convert opinion and fears into substantive facts we can work with.)

Understand the meaning behind
the words we hear.

Our Follow-up Questions will naturally move their response from

GENERAL to SPECIFIC

Our questions will convert:

Opinions
Assumptions
Misunderstanding
Fears

Into

Facts
Meaning
Clarity
Honesty

Now I understand.

To recap: A clearer picture emerges with just a few follow-up questions. *What* and *how* questions can help unwrap a person's thinking. The next question is found from a *keyword* within their previous answer. Each follow-up question will gift more clarity with each response.

Questions conveniently move meaning from general to specific. The follow-up process converts opinions, assumptions, misunderstandings, and fears into facts, substance, and options we can reasonably discuss without misunderstanding.

TIP: Be sensitive with curiosity. Too many rapid-fire questions can annoy and shut down the recipient.

Many things are lost for want of not asking. - English Proverb

Chapter 8

Test Questions

Knowledge never enters the head through an open mouth.

Surveying the Soundness of an Idea

Test questions are akin to follow-up questions asked *beforehand* or *afterward* to survey the thinking around a subject before voicing our opinion. Test questions compare others' thinking to our own without debate. A simple inquiry might highlight errors that hadn't been considered, helping make better choices for ourselves and others.

Asking Beforehand

Michael, a team leader, has a department proposal. Before implementing, he invites his team to a meeting and asks, "What is your thinking around merging the two departments?" It may take more time upfront, but he will gain valuable information to adjust his idea to encourage group buy-in and support.

Telling people our decision before testing the attitudes around that decision may silence pertinent information. *"I'm going to institute the marketing group's plan ASAP."* My direct statement may provoke complaints, silence, indifference, or defiance. Instead say, *"What's your thinking around the marketing group's plan?"* or *"What do you like most and least about their ideas?"* Test the waters by encouraging others to share their insights and attitudes instead of prematurely forcing our decision. *"What do you think needs to happen to implement this program?"* We may even hear a better approach or uncover something we've missed.

People want to feel involved and have input in the process of change. There is a sense of safety and security in understanding the change that is about to affect us.

Reframe our declaration of intent (*"I'm going to..."* or *"We're going to..."*) into a test question by asking:

> *"What is your thinking around ...?"*
>
> *"What if we were to ...?"*
>
> *"How about if we try...?"*
>
> *"What will happen if we ...?"*
>
> *"What do you see as the downside to ...?"*

Asking Afterwards

Asking test questions afterward is equally effective. The host of the popular TV show *Who Wants to Be a Millionaire*, Regis Philbin, would verify the contestant's answer by asking, *"Is that your final answer?"* The decision goes back to the contestant to reconsider and confirm.

When we communicate, *telling* versus *asking* yields two different outcomes. Telling someone their idea or actions are wrong awaken doubt and emotions by challenging their self-interest and dignity. Instead, ask questions to test the rationale behind their position, *"How did you come to a decision?"* We create a dialogue instead of debate, perhaps bringing forward something they haven't considered. Our questions convey a sense of curiosity *and* test the rationale and soundness of their decision.

Situation	Test Question to Ask
An unpopular decision is made.	*"What is the downside to this decision?"*
Adamant about their choice.	*"What other options have been considered?"*
Make big changes to a department.	*"What effect will that have on the team?"*
Impulsive decision to be made.	*"What happens if we wait?"*
Decision directly affects you.	*"What if I'm unable to do that, then what?"*

Whether at home or work, we disagree with many decisions people make, particularly when they affect us. Navigating terrible choices can be touchy. The temptation is to plunge in with our fixes, opinions, conclusions, or proposals. Instead of challenging, **convert concerns** into test questions. *"How will that affect such and such?" "What will happen if...?" "What if we try...?"* Draw out their response further with follow-up questions. *"How do you mean?" "For example?"* The exchange continues by asking questions instead of making direct statements. Perhaps we may inspire a better understanding for a mutually beneficial outcome.

To know one thing, we must know the opposite. - Henry Moore

Resolving Questions

*A chip on the shoulder is about
the heaviest load that anyone can carry.*

We get provoked. We restrain ourselves as much as possible. Our emotions get pushed further, and we finally assert what *we* believe is right. Positions solidify as the volume increases. Words turn personal, and civility is extinguished. Pride takes a firm stance, and we both walk away frustrated. If only we could talk it through sensibly. Again, when the emotions are high, the ability to listen and reason is low.

Just because our opponent is a quick thinker, fast talker, or speaks louder does not make them right. We *both* want our say yet will be denied until we take the higher ground. We do so by setting aside our pride and righteousness long enough to Acknowledge (**A**), Clarify (**C**), then Talk (**T**). If not, we get stuck arguing the same issue over and over. If emotions begin to intensify beyond comfort, we can postpone a meaningful conversation until emotions calm (See Setting Boundaries on page 27).

"Justin corners me, saying he wants his ideas respected around a joint work project. I've heard this before from him. Even though I think I'm treating Justin respectfully, he doesn't think so. Voices get louder as feelings ignite. We both think we're right, talking over each other to justify our position. Neither listens. Finally, I say enough is enough and walk away exasperated thinking that Justin is wrong."

An Invitation to Reconcile

No one was ever crucified for asking the right question.

What if our issue *is* necessary to resolve? At what point do we find a resolution *after* an argument? When *the benefit* to reconcile outweighs *the cost of pride*. It is not about giving in or giving up to *unjustly* accommodate. We have a better choice.

Time has passed to reflect. My emotions are calm, and my thinking is clear. I decide to settle the issue. What do I do? Re-engage by invitation. **Present my invitation to the preferred future outcome that we both want.** *"Are you interested in finding a way we can work better together on this project?"* My invitation addresses the issue <u>neutrally</u>, allowing everyone to save face. The worst we can hear is a, *"No."* If so, follow with, *"What makes you say that?"* We transfer the explanation to their shoulders and still keep the door open. If *"Yes,"* we agree to meet in person, by phone, or virtually. What if we hear, *"There is no problem here."* Denial or pride may be too strong to move forward at this time. We can re-ask at a later date when the issue becomes more obvious to their interest.

Our invitation to reconcile, which is <u>not neutral</u>, can draw contention quickly. *"Let's meet, but if you are going to be angry like our last conversation, I'll wait until you deal with your anger."* Our invite points to a fault and refers to the past. Exclude any implied threat of blame, judgment, shame, criticism, or assumptions. When properly asked, our invitation to meet gets the thinking around the problem pointed in the right direction, towards a working solution.

After thinking about what happened between Justin and me this morning, I decided to resolve this issue. I thought, "Until I clarify what he means by respect, we will continue to argue. We must work together on this project with the deadline approaching." I walked up to Justin and asked, "Are you willing to find a way we can work better together?" He said, "Yes." I then asked, "Is this a good time to talk?"

He nodded. I acknowledged first by saying, "I'm hearing you'd like me to treat your ideas more respectfully than I have." He says, "Yes!" Emotions relaxed, and a civil conversation began. I asked, "May I ask a few questions to understand better?" He replied, "Okay." I continued with a resolving question, "Justin, what would be treating your ideas more respectfully look like?" He quickly responded, "Stop being so critical and disagreeing with my every thought and idea."

I followed with, "How do you want me to express any concerns?" Justin said, "Work together with me. I need you to explain why you feel my idea is not beneficial and discuss the options. We're working together on this project, and both our insights are valuable." I finally got it and said, "Fair enough, I can do that." By asking a few questions to clarify, instead of defending, we exposed all the facts and needs making it much easier to talk it out without blame. We now have a better understanding of how to negotiate differences with future issues.

Reconcile Ongoing Issues with Resolving Questions

Below are examples of resolving questions to begin a conversation on various issues when we meet:

Issue	Sample Resolving Question
Relationship:	*What does a good relationship look like to you?*
Teamwork:	*What does good teamwork look like to you?*
Housework:	*What does fairness in doing housework look like?*
Vacation:	*What does a great vacation look like to you?*
Respect:	*What actions let you know you're being respected?*
Working Together:	*What does working better together look like to you?*
Marriage:	*What does a good marriage look like for you?*
Loyalty:	*What does loyalty look like to you?*
Independence:	*What does working independently look like to you?*
Managing Others:	*How do you best like to be managed?*
Sensitive Person:	*How shall I communicate a difficult subject with you?*
Ornery Teenager:	*How do you want me to talk to you so that both of us are heard?*

Allie and I were recently married. Like most couples, we have adjustments to make. Allie accused me of not doing my share around the house. She came home stressed after a long day at work, walked into the kitchen, and said to me, "You never do the dishes!" I defended myself, saying, "I do the dishes all the time." Into a fray, we went. My defensiveness prevented me from listening or acknowledging what she said. I was offended. We parted the room. While I was stewing, I thought: This issue has occurred between us before. I want to solve this problem. I know the dishes are a trigger for something else she wants or needs.

It was uncommonly quiet the following day before we left for work. I texted later that day and asked, "Want to find a way we can get our fair share of chores done around the house without debate? Want to talk after work?"

*She texted back and accepted **the invitation.** I thought about our issue throughout the day and asked myself, "What values or real needs are most likely at stake for Allie?" (See page 16 for a list of values and needs.) I concluded, fairness and order. Fairness is important to me, as well. Order, not so much.*

*That evening, we sat on the couch with pen and paper in hand. I first said, "I could have handled myself better than I did last night. For that, I'm sorry." She added, "I'm sorry, too." The atmosphere changed. **I then acknowledged,** "Fairness seems important to you, Allie." "Yes," she replied. "May I ask you a question?" She said, "Yes." I resumed and **asked a resolving question,** "What would doing our fair share of chores around the house look like to you?" She calmly replied, "We each do our part." I knew there was more to her answer, so I followed with "And?" She added, "We pick up after ourselves." Again, I followed with, "What else?" The list grew. **I summarized** what she said. I finally had a clear picture of the crucial pieces that defined what doing our fair share meant to her. Now, we can discuss.*

*I picked one of her points and asked for her definition, "Allie, you said we each do our part. What does that look like to you?" Wow! She had a vivid description and examples of who would do what and when. It was easy to agree. "I agree, yet I would like to add …" We talked back and forth to fine-tune the first agreement. There was more on the list. **I picked another point** she made for further clarification, and asked, "What do you mean by we pick up after ourselves? I know I'm somewhat messy and leave things on the floor." We laughed and talked through my messiness as I promised to work on it. We had such an honest conversation. Our relationship broke new ground. Who would think arguing over dirty dishes would end up here? We both defined and agreed on what was truly fair and vital to both of us, our marriage, and how to manage the household tasks best. We grew closer.*

Conversations run more smoothly when we are not defending who is right and who is wrong. *"I now know what Allie meant after complaining about the dishes. So much was hidden behind the words* *she used. It helped to break the issue down into its <u>most basic parts</u> and then discussed each part separately."*

Summary of The Steps to Resolve

Re-engage by inviting a conversation around the <u>general preferred future outcome</u> that both of us want. *"Are you interested in finding ways we can strengthen our relationship?"* We can re-engage anytime, now or in the future.

When we meet, open with a resolving question that best fits the issue at hand. Base our question on the *general* result that we both want when resolved. *"What does a good relationship look like to you?"* Then listen.

Build a list from their answer. Follow with *"And?"* regardless of the initial response to our question. Continue with another *"And?"* or *"What else?"* until we have two, three, or four items that make up their <u>*complete definition*</u> of the resolving question. Doing so breaks down the issue into smaller specific topics to discuss. The more points we have on the list, the more focused and thorough talk becomes.

Summarize the points we heard and conclude with: *"Is there anything else to add?"* Once the definition is complete and precise, we offer ours. *"This is how I define a good working relationship."* In our description, avoid using the *"you shouldn't," "you can't," "you don't," "you never"* language when offering our definition. Those words tend to point blame and push buttons (See page 75 for a list of words). Put our points in terms of **what I want** versus what I don't want or like them to do.

Pick <u>ONE</u> of the points and talk. Highlight the areas where we share common ground and clarify areas that differ. Ask follow-up questions when necessary. Discuss each item *separately* until resolved. If the discussion hits a snag, pick another point on the list and continue. *"Let's move on to another point and get back to this one later."* Often, resolving one issue on the list will help us clarify previously discussed or other listed points.

> **TIP:** Uncommonly, we will encounter someone who responds frivolously. For example, we ask, *"How do you best like to work with others?"* They respond, *"I don't!"* Immediately follow with, *"And?"* If we hear the same response, ask, *"How is that going to help us work together?"* We want to build an honest list. If not, they are not taking the issue seriously, or there may be a larger problem underneath.

When one will not, two cannot resolve.

Chapter 10

Special Situations

*It is an illusion to think that we win
by trying to make the other person wrong.*

Stuck in The Past? Move to The Future

Sometimes our conversation gets stuck in the past by repeating over and over what has already happened. Blame begins to assert itself. Unresolved emotions and pride keep us locked in a battle over **The Past**.

We know we're in the past when we hear the finger-pointing language of **you** did **what** to **whom** and **who** is right. Reconciliation is difficult and emotionally draining when we rehash what has already happened. On the reverse side, solutions work on how we would like **The Future** to be. Resolving is *who* will **agree** to do *what* by *when, where,* and *how.*

Where is The Conversation Focused?

The Past — Emotional ———————— Conversational → **The Future**

The Past	The Future
• Focuses on Problem.	• Focuses on Solutions.
• Who did What to Whom.	• Who will agree to do What by When, Where and How.
• Emotions often triggered.	• Agreements made.
• When stuck in the past something is unresolved.	

When we get stuck arguing *who is right* and *who is wrong,* progress is at a standstill. The past emphasizes: *You don't, You can't, and You should not,* bringing the twelve button-pushing words (See page 75) into the conversation. If the conversation gets stuck in the past, we can encourage moving forward by asking:

"Let's focus on what we can do instead of can't do."

"Instead of what you don't want, what actions do you want?"

"What do you need to happen to move forward?"

"How do you wish it was?"

"Is it in both our interests to resolve this?"

"If this problem continues, then what?"

Answers to any of the above questions will lead us to our next step: to continue, call a time-out to cool down, or postpone the discussion for another time.

When stuck in the past, emotional and personal considerations remain unresolved, blocking resolution. If our attempt to resolve ends in an impasse, we have accomplished far more than leaving the issues mute, keeping the door open for a future discussion.

If a problem has no solution, it may not be a problem -
but simply a fact to be tolerated. - Shimon Peres

Fixed Positions and Questions

The battle between opposite forces exists in everything. - Sir Isaac Newton

Ever try to change someone's mind from a deeply held opinion or belief? Confronting a person's view usually invites resistance. We do not all think alike or interpret the same information in the same way. Most people will get angry and refuse to reply to our question when asked sneeringly, *"Why on earth would you believe that?"* Telling people they're wrong does not change their minds.

Instead, ask a follow-up question after their comment without being *suggestive, leading, indirect,* or *assumptive.* Invite clarification without confrontation. *"What makes you say that?"* Display curiosity about what led to their thinking. Follow up with *what* and *how* questions. Upon further inquiry, more common ground may be found than previously thought.

If their answers still make little sense, test <u>their openness to listen</u> with an acknowledgment, *"I hear this view is important to you."* Follow with the question, *"What would it take to be open to a different view?"* If they say, *"Nothing will!"* Take them at their word and stop engaging. The emotions are too entrenched for a meaningful conversation. Any attempt to force our views can quickly deteriorate into a test of wills trying to prove each other wrong.

We find it difficult to admit we're wrong, even when presented with facts. If we perceive no incentive to change our perspective, there is little chance we will. We have a choice. **How much time, effort, and energy do we expend disproving their point of view in favor of our own?** Our best option is to agree to disagree and move on without argument. We change when we're ready.

We can be right and still lose the fight.

√ In our world of dualistic thinking *(yes/no, up/down, right/ wrong, hot/cold, left/right)*, the opposition between viewpoints is natural. No one viewpoint has a monopoly on reality. Communication has *at least* two sides—ours and theirs.

√ When we ask the *right kind* of question at the *right time*, we invite someone to expand upon their perspective. Thus, it allows us to *adjust* our response to more accurate information.

√ Ask follow-up questions **after** someone says something, inviting an elaboration on what they meant. Like a magnifying glass, we see their meaning more clearly. **Any term used to respond is open and reasonable territory for a follow-up question.**

√ Follow-up questions are *neutral.* There is nothing *suggestive, leading, indirect,* or *assumptive* built into the question when asked. Thus, we exclude any influence upon the person's answer.

√ Test questions are akin to follow-up questions asked *beforehand* or *afterward* to survey the thinking around a subject before voicing our opinion. Test questions compare others' thinking to our own without debate.

√ Navigating terrible choices can be tricky. The temptation is to plunge in with our fixes, opinions, conclusions, or proposals. Instead of challenging, convert that temptation over our concerns into a test question.

√ Sometimes our conversation gets stuck in the past by repeating over and over what has already happened. Unresolved emotions and pride keep us locked in a battle over **The Past.**

√ How much *time, effort,* and *energy* do we expend disproving their point of view in favor of our own?

PART THREE
Talk

The A.C.T. Way to Respond to Everyday Communication Without Argument

Acknowledge   **Clarify**   **Talk**

Emotional   Conversational

Emotional Zone
Calm emotions by validating
their experience to let them
know they were heard.

Discovery Zone
Ask the right question
to clarify their view
before sharing ours.

Discussion Zone
Talk it out and work
towards a solution.
(What + Why + How)

Strong emotions compromise the ability to reason and listen.

Copyright © 2021 Mark Ortman

Choosing Our Words Wisely

If people can take things the wrong way, they will. - Murphy's law

Words have the power to help, heal, hurt, or inspire. How we state *what we want* or *mean* makes a difference. Would it differ if we heard, *"All I see in you is <u>wasted</u> potential,"* versus *"All I see in you is <u>tremendous</u> potential?"* Each statement conveys the same thing except for one word, leading to a critical slant on the meaning and interpretation.

In everyday communication, we employ two terms from linguistics: syntax and diction. The syntax is <u>our arrangement of words in a sentence</u>. Diction refers to <u>our choice of words</u>. In combination, both help us develop the tone, mood, and atmosphere from our statements—written or spoken. When we rearrange the words, we change the effect. We can influence whether we elicit resistance, hard feelings, or accord.

Communication Defined

Not getting the result we want? Usually, our *approach* or their *interpretation* is often the culprit. Thus, we will define communication as: The *effects* our words have on others.

Communication defined:
The *effects* our words have on others.

Fact vs Perception

When we speak or write, everyday communication shares up to six topics (in combination): The **Who, When, Where, What, Why,** and **How.**

The **Who, When,** and **Where** typically carries or confirms a fact. *"I'm going to the five o'clock meeting." "Sam and I went to the movies last night." "I ran into Kayla yesterday."* When the facts lack sufficient detail, or we are curious for more information, respond with a follow-up question to clarify. *"What did Kayla have to say?"*

On the other hand, when we state **What** we want or know, **Why** it is of value, or instructions on **How** to do something, we impart our point of view *(perspective, priorities, bias, opinions, interests, wants, and desires).* Thus, our statement can challenge the way others see things, which can quickly lead to misunderstanding and disagreement.

Fact Arena Who / When / Where Expresses Facts
Perception Arena What / Why / How Expresses Views

Part 3 will outline various ways to say what we mean to increase the probability that our words are straightforward and convincing. The goal of this chapter is to learn to express what we want or know without having to force our idea or the outcome. Ever see a sports team, company, or household *demoralized* into victory? Over the long haul, our positive respectful language will yield far better results than a pushy forceful advance.

The three skills include:

1 How to be positive yet direct when stating **WHAT** we want.

2 How to open others to our viewpoint with the right reason **WHY.**

3 How to explain with tact and influence **HOW** we want to see something done.

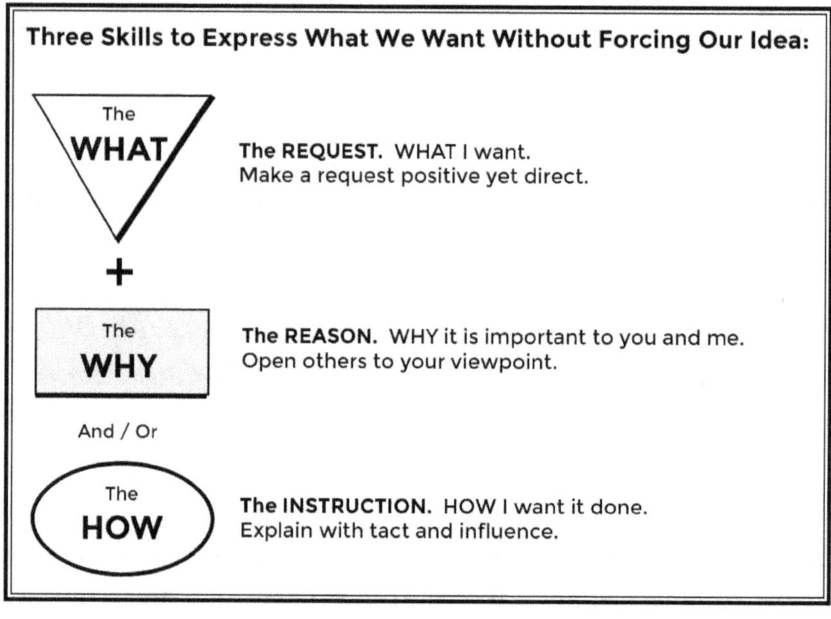

Three Skills to Express What We Want Without Forcing Our Idea:

The
WHAT

+

The
WHY

And / Or

The
HOW

The REQUEST. WHAT I want.
Make a request positive yet direct.

The REASON. WHY it is important to you and me.
Open others to your viewpoint.

The INSTRUCTION. HOW I want it done.
Explain with tact and influence.

Chapter 12

The WHAT

When fear is introduced by another, the motive is usually control.

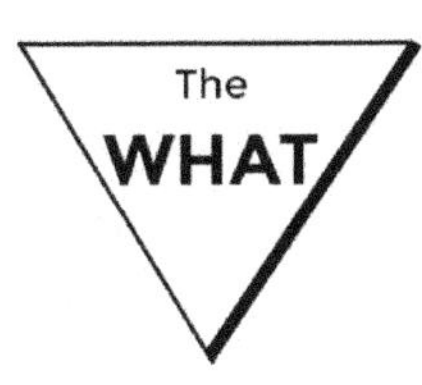

Our words (written or spoken) help us get what we want. Throughout the day, we make numerous requests. We tell our son to clean up after himself, we email a colleague for an updated report, we ask our boss for additional resources needed for a project. How we word what we want helps determine whether we get resistance or cooperation. It is not about being *too nice*. It is about being *skillful* with our approach.

Forcing someone to conform to our ideals is no way to inspire collaboration. A few may succumb to the pressure and eventually grow weary of our ill-mannered tactics and push back.

Make a Request Positive Yet Direct

People hear statements more literally (without misconstruing) when we state *what they can do* or *what I want* versus *what they can't do* or *what I don't like*. For example, if I tell someone what they can't do, we may open them to wonder *"Why not?"* or the defiant, *"I'll do what I want"* or the confused, *"I'm not certain what to do."* These response add unintended rivalry to our request.

Using the word *"don't"* in our request may challenge the receiver to take an extra mental step to sort the meaning of the statement. *"Please don't remain seated."* We may interpret correctly and stand up, yet may require a moment of thought wondering *why*.

On the other hand, stating what we _do want_ is more straight-forward. _"Please stand."_ The brain knows what was requested by being precise and direct (using fewer words).

How do I make my request positive yet direct? **Convert what we don't want or like into what we do want.** We state the favorable outcome or action we seek. For example, _"Don't leave the door open when you leave"_ can be converted to _"Close the door when you leave."_ Others will hear our request more succinctly and clearly without overthinking how it was said or what was said.

Using criticism _(What I don't like)_ to get what we want is _indirect_ and invites justification instead of cooperation. For example, _"You never clean up after yourself!"_ does not clearly state what I want. It implies blame leaving the other to justify or defend, _"What do you mean I never? You always leave a mess, too!"_ Back and forth we go, distancing our desired outcome. _"You never clean up after yourself!"_ voices **what they did that I don't like** rather than **what I want.** Frame our request into the favorable outcome or action we seek. _"Please clean up when finished."_ Instead of triggering justification, we get cooperation or a discussion that leaves emotion out of the picture. If we state our desire _indirectly_ with criticism, then what we want may be delayed from refuting.

> **TIP:** Convert our request from _what we don't want_ or _like_ **into** _what we do want_ by stating the _favorable outcome we seek_ or _what specific action_ we want the other to take.

Negative vs Positive Requests

It is easy for our words to run _counter_ to what we want. When _we lead with our frustration,_ we usually _default_ into _the negative._ Our terms become critical or judgmental and risk pushing people's buttons. For example:

Negative Request	**Positive, Direct Request**
What we DON'T want.	The outcome or action we DO want.
"Why can't you stop being so negative?"	*"Tell me the positives."*
"Can't you stop yelling all the time?"	*"Talk to me in a calm voice."*
"You always leave me out of the loop."	*"I would appreciate being included."*
"You always talk behind my back."	*"Talk directly to me if you have a concern."*
"You can't do that."	*"Try this."*
"You never put the mail on the counter."	*"Please leave the mail on the counter."*
"You spend too much time at work."	*"Please come home early tomorrow."*
"You never spend time with the children."	*"Please spend time with the children."*
"Don't get sick."	*"Stay healthy."*

A story to illustrate how choosing my words wisely matters: *When I transferred to my new job, I moved into a top-floor unit of a two-story apartment building. The next day, someone moved in below. On Monday at 7:00 a.m. sharp, I heard a loud slam from the unit downstairs. The heavy solid wood doors shook my apartment, startling me. I wondered if this was normal for the new neighbor or if he was just in a hurry. Tuesday at 7:00 a.m. sharp, he slammed the front door again. I could feel my frustration mount. Of course, I could start slamming my door in retaliation, though that would diminish any peaceful outcome. Instead, I thought to myself, "How can I ask him to stop slamming the door every morning without creating defensiveness?"*

*I was prepared for Wednesday morning. At 7:00 a.m. he left his unit, again slamming the door. I called out from the open kitchen window above as he walked by to his car, "Excuse me, I am your neighbor above. **Would you kindly close your front door more gently when you leave? Those doors are heavy and make a lot of noise."** He looked up at me with a blank stare for a moment, probably retracing his steps in his mind, and said, "Sure." I said, "Thanks," and he walked off.*

Note, I framed my request into the favorable **outcome** *and* **action** *that I wanted. Thursday morning was the test. He closed his door gently. Friday, the door was quietly closed. Saturday morning, I knocked on his door to introduce myself and thanked him again, reinforcing my request. Problem solved.*

We usually do things out of *habit, interests,* and *convenience* more so than malicious intent. People are generally reasonable and accommodating when respectfully addressed. Had I said, *"For crying out loud, can't you stop slamming your front door!"* I imply blame or challenge undermining what I want, whether I am accurate or not.

A sharp tongue can cut our own throat. - Confucius

Twelve Words That Push People's Buttons

I've been "should" upon long enough!

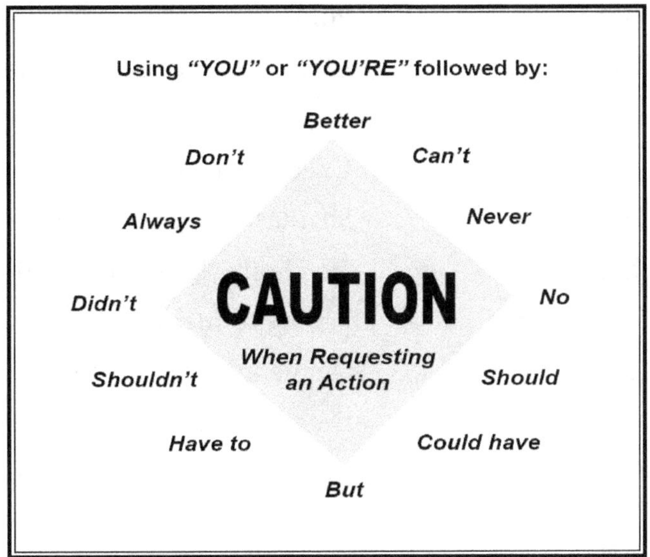

Misusing the twelve words risks pushing people's buttons. Growing up, we have heard our parents tell us what *we should* and *can't do,* placing limits and restrictions on our actions. As adults, that <u>controlling language</u> is outdated. At times it may work. However, we test the sensitivity of the recipient and may spark an emotional reaction.

When <u>requesting an action</u>, be cautious when leading our statement with the word **you** or **you're,** followed by one of the twelve words that push people's buttons. When we *blame, criticize,* or *judge* someone's behavior, the twelve words are commonly present. We imply, *"You're wrong, and you should do it my way,"* inciting justification or defensiveness.

There are many ways to interpret the twelve words that push people's buttons; thus, lies the danger. For example:

We Say	Possible Interpretation
You better…	Offers up a threat.
You're never…	A generalization that belittles.
You don't…	Points finger. Blames.
You can't…	Limits options. Underestimates.
You're always…	A generalization that exaggerates.
You shouldn't…	Unsolicited advice that shames.
You didn't…	Shames. Invites justification.
You have to…	No choice. Eliminates options.
You should have…	Failure to measure up.
You could have…	Challenges the choice we made.
But	Discounts what previously said.
No	Invites debate if we disagree.

The twelve words can confuse our intent. When used, we find they push our *opinion, preference, judgment,* or *frustration* onto others.

Use the more direct approach to urge action by stating *what we want* instead of *what we don't want* or *like.* Leave these twelve words out of our request. "*Please take the trash out by 6 p.m. to ensure it's collected.*" Clearly state what is desired without making the recipient feel judged.

> **TIP:** The twelve words are okay for everyday use when *explaining, responding,* or *summarizing.* "*I can't make it to the meeting tonight.*" "*I could have saved time driving instead of taking the bus.*" "*I always seem to miss the best parties.*" "*What I'm hearing you say is…*"

Remember that you will never get ahead of somebody as long as you are kicking them in the seat of the pants. - Walter Winchell

Chapter 13

The WHY

People do things for their reasons when they see value in doing so.

Open Others to Our Point of View

The **WHY**

Are we primarily interested in ourselves? Would that make us selfish? Not necessarily. The first law of nature is the law of *self-preservation*. We use that instinct to survive. Thus, self-interest is baked into our decision-making. When we make everyday choices, we weigh our desires, needs, wants, interests, what we gain, or lose, and at what cost. In other words, we ask ourselves, *"How will this choice affect (or benefit) me or what I care about?"*

Olivia made her first presentation at a vendor meeting. All the decision-makers were present. Her purpose was to sway her client into switching to an updated billing process introduced by her company. She spent endless hours preparing beforehand. After her twenty minute presentation, questions followed. A few days later, her client declined the new billing procedure. She felt dejected. She talked to her client and discovered she fell short in explaining the reasons why the new product is better at satisfying her client's needs over the current option. She went back to the drawing board, researched, and translated the new product benefits to pinpoint her client's interests and needs more accurately. In other words, she shared why it's important to them, and how they would save and benefit from upgrading compared to what they were currently using. Olivia learned a valuable lesson.

When encountering hesitancy or objections to our appeal or proposal, the reason *why* is often in question. When reasons are weak, resistance will follow. Consider asking a test question to disclose more information. *"What do you like most (or least) about this idea?"* What was missed may be disclosed. Talk becomes more open and honest when all the reasons *why* are on the table. Work toward a solution that ideally satisfies both parties (Win/Win). Hidden agendas and vested interests may leave relevant facts out of the discussion. An agreement may be undermined where someone wins at the expense of the other (Win/Lose).

The Importance of WHAT + WHY

People are not against you,
they are merely for themselves. - Gene Fowler

We've all heard our parents tell us to do something as a kid. We ask, *"Why?"* They respond, *"Because I said so!"* Although disingenuous, that is a reason since it provides an explanation. When still left wondering why, defiance could become a temptation. People have their actual reasons, whether willing to share or not. The true motive may be concealed beneath the given reason *"why."*

Conviction is strengthened when we know *why* we are doing something. The stronger the reason, the greater our conviction. I go on a diet because I want to be healthier. I want my daughter home by 10:00 p.m. over safety concerns. I request something because I have a goal of finishing on time.

We usually comply with requests when interests align or make sense to us. *"On your way home, will you pick up some milk (what) so we can make pancakes for breakfast (why)?"* If I am interested in having pancakes for breakfast, I will remember the milk. The strength of the motive ensures follow through.

Excluding the *"why"* from *"what we want"* leaves the other person to conclude its importance. Communicate the *"what"* plus the *"why"* that contains the **purpose, benefit,** or **vision** behind our request.

*My friend John visits after being on the road for ten days. He asks if he can wash his clothes. "Sure, the detergent is in the cupboard above the washing machine. Fill it to the black line around the cap for each load." He acknowledges, "Okay." A half-hour later, the buzzer goes off. The wash is done. John walks into the laundry room, and I hear, "Holy sh**!" That got my attention! I ran to the room and noticed the suds all over the floor and the machine. "How much detergent did you use?" I yelped. He justifies, "The machine was so stuffed with my dirty clothes I didn't think it was enough soap, so I put three capfuls." He cleaned up the mess and rewashed his clothes to get the excess suds out. Would the outcome have changed had I included a **why** with the **what**? "Fill the detergent to the black line around the cap (what) because it is highly concentrated. A little goes a long way" (why)." Probably.*

We also get **comfort** and **certainty** in knowing the *reason why.* Our mental and emotional well-being are served instead of being left in the dark. We may feel uncomfortable asking *why* and silently draw our conclusions, which may differ from the reality of the situation. For example:

Driving home one evening, I heard a siren and saw flashing lights through my rearview mirror. I immediately thought, "Why am I being pulled over? I'm driving the speed limit." I pulled to the side of the road and stopped. The police car pulled up behind me. The officer came to my car window and asked for my license and registration.

Tension mounted inside of me. He asked me to leave my engine idling with my lights on and step out of the car. My heart was pounding. He leads me to the back of my car, pointed, and said, "Your tail light is out." He advised me to get it fixed, smiled, and sent me on my way. What a relief knowing WHY I was being pulled over.

Why We Change Our Minds

Where there is interest, there is energy.

Have we ever changed our minds after uncovering new information that **serves our interests better than our prior choice?**

I called my brother in Phoenix a couple of weeks before my semi-annual visit to arrange an airport pickup. I timed this trip around my niece's seventh birthday in late September. As we were talking on the phone, my brother mentioned, "Taylor wants to take piano lessons, and I'm going to get an upright piano for the back room for her birthday." I responded, "Great! Have you considered a synthesizer?" He said, "No, I'm getting an upright piano." I persisted with, "Taylor can get all kinds of piano sounds from a synthesizer." He insists, "I'm getting an upright piano!" We changed the subject to what we were going to do during my visit, then I sneaked in, "You know an electric piano would be easier to move around." He stated, "Drop it, Mark!" I disregarded his frustration and threw out one last thought lingering at the tip of my tongue, "Taylor can practice with headphones." A moment of silence, followed by a chuckle. He responded, "I didn't think of that. Tell me more about the electric piano."

Upon arrival at the airport, my brother was waiting. After a quick bite to eat, we stopped at the piano store to purchase a Yamaha electric keyboard with headphones. Was he thinking of his interest?

In everyday disagreements, people get stuck quibbling over the "what" without asking "why." I apologized for my persistence. He thanked me for my idea.

I got lucky to find the incentive that resonated with my brother's interest. The headphone idea satisfied a real need he had *not* considered, the value of **comfort** through peace and quiet!

Find the Right Reason WHY

We do things for a reason. In general, we seek to *gain, save, have, be, feel, know,* and *experience* something that <u>satisfies</u> our real needs and values (see page 16). Once we agree with the reason, we act without resistance. Our motive resides in the *"why."* **Make it easy for others to see how serving our interests serves theirs.**

When we want to know where **others'** interests lay, we learn by *asking, listening,* or *knowing* them. Three examples to illustrate:

1 <u>**Find THEIR reasons WHY**</u>. When the right questions are asked, answers are revealed. *"What are you looking for in the proposal that's most important to you?" "How will that be of value?" "What will it take to get this done?"* Have a conversation. Connect. Invite answers without pressure. **Discover what's truly important to them.** Understand their needs and rationale. More common ground may exist than previously thought. When we help fulfill their interest, they will help meet ours. This differs from manipulating or bribing because with mutual interests satisfied, both win!

2 <u>**Ask Test Questions**</u>. Reasons are not as hidden as we thought. Instead of making a direct statement, convert our request into a test question **built on the desired result.** *"What do you think if we move the table over there?" "What do you think if we raise our prices by 5%?"* Learn what they think, and if it differs, discuss it. **Listening** to their words will reveal their interest, needs, values, and emotions. The conversation continues with fresh insight.

3 <u>**Share WHY it is important to me.**</u> I say, *"It will save me loads of time and effort."* The risk is that my reason might not carry enough incentive (i.e., they don't care) to gain their support. We help support people we care about or like and see value in doing so. The better we **know someone**, the easier it is to be familiar and share our interests that align with theirs.

> **TIP:** When someone badgers us to do something, and we are hesitant, conclude their persistence by saying: *"Let me think about that"* or *" I'll look that over."* It doesn't commit us to agreement or disagreement yet signals we may be willing to consider options before moving forward. Another option is to inquire. *"Help me understand what makes this so important to you?"*

What attracts our interest, holds our attention.

Chapter 14

The HOW

If we have been put in our place long enough,
we begin to act like the place. - Randall Jarrell

Explain with Tact

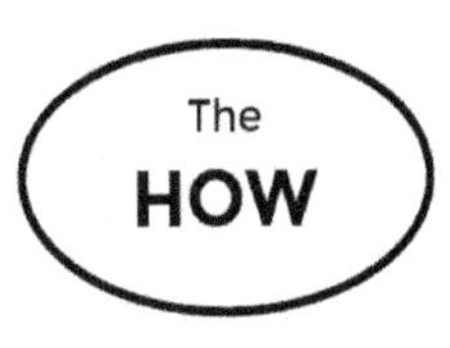

Mason is new at his job and is still learning the ropes. His supervisor approaches and notices Mason doing his task incorrectly. Without checking in with Mason, he barks, "You're doing it all wrong!" Mason is embarrassed, as he thought he was doing it correctly.

Instead, what would happen if the supervisor said, *"Hey Mason, company policy requires us to do it this way because of safety procedures and insurance liability." Now Mason understands the WHAT + WHY and does not feel ashamed for not knowing. He is more open to being coached on HOW to accomplish the task. A change in our approach costs us nothing yet helps us be heard, furthering trust and collaboration in the relationship. Mason now knows about the policy without being told he was wrong.*

When we explain **HOW** to do something, give advice, state our view, or coach for improvement, draw from personal experiences. Choose examples from: *"how **I** do it"* or *"how **I** notice **others** (they know or respect) do it"* or *"how the policy manual, regulation, or situation require us to do it."* Include the What + Why. We might say, *"I found turning left on Forest Street (What) will save time and bypass the heavy traffic and construction (Why)."* Our words are more convincing.

This way, we keep the often finger-pointing word *"you"* (followed by one of the other twelve words that push buttons) from complicating intent. When we begin our statement with the word *"you,"* we sound like we're blaming, criticizing, demeaning, or trying to parent someone's behavior, *"You can't do it that way."* Change our focus from how **you should** see it **or** do it **to** how *I* do it **or** how **others** do it. *"Jenny told me she found it easier doing it this way."* Adding a good reason *why*, makes the *how* easier and clearer for others to hear (and cooperate).

Influence with Tact

> *It is harder to lead someone further than we have gone.* - Gene Mauch

I moved to be closer to my brother, who lived 120 miles away. Looking to get a long-overdue dental cleaning, I asked him if he knew a good dentist in town. He responded, "I go to Dr. Jane." He added, "Ask for Nancy to clean your teeth. She is thorough." I called the dental office and made an appointment with Nancy. Thorough was an understatement. She spent seventy-five minutes cleaning my teeth in what was a forty-five minute appointment! Ouch!

After several years of seeing Nancy as my hygienist, she noticed very little plaque on my teeth during a recent cleaning. Being curious, she asked, "Are you flossing regularly?" I responded, "Only before I have an appointment with you!" She chuckled and followed with, "Any changes in your dental or diet routine?" I said, "I bought a tongue scraper and used it daily." She responded, "Tongue scrapers are great because they take the bacteria off your tongue that cause plaque and tartar buildup." It begged the question, "How were my brother's plaque and tartar from his appointment last week?" She smiled, not to violate confidentiality. I read her non-verbal queue as he had a lot of plaque.

My brother came over the next week and asked how my appointment was with "thorough Nancy?" I told him, "It was the easiest and most pain-free cleaning I've ever had with her."

"What changed?" he asked. "I bought a tongue scraper, and she said it takes the bacteria off the tongue that causes plaque and tartar buildup on the teeth."

The following week I went to visit my brother. I used the bathroom and noticed a tongue scraper on the counter. I said, "You bought a tongue scraper." He nodded, "Yes." I never told my brother to buy one. People do things for their reasons when they see value in doing so.

Our experiences influence when they share the other person's interests. If our example serves up the right incentive, they act without being forced to do so. Interested in a tongue scraper?

Explain *"how"* to do something by prefacing with **I, for me,** or **others have found**. We reduce the direct implication, *"you are wrong,"* from our words. Choose personal examples that *serve their interest* by connecting to their level of awareness. If our understanding differs, our approach keeps the door open for discussion.

I, for me, or others have found vs. "you" language

Opinion	**Factual**
("You" language)	(Direct experiences)
"You should exercise more."	*"<u>I found</u> exercise helps reduce my stress."*
"I feel you should do it like this."	*"<u>For me,</u> it saves time doing it this way."*
"You're doing it all wrong."	*"<u>Linda said</u> she gets the best results by ..."*
"You can't do it that way."	*"The <u>policy manual</u> requires we ..."*

Leading with the word *"you"* creates distance by pointing our finger at the other person for what they *did* or *do*. Preferably, share the positive outcome we desire. We are more apt to be perceived as helpful instead of being accusatory. The commanding *"You should..."* or *"You can't..."* or *"I feel you should..."* sounds like unsolicited advice, criticism, or an aggressive demand.

Instead, share a personal insight that is valuable and inspiring. Sharing from *"I"* makes our suggestion easier to hear and less dictatorial. Adults prefer to make their own decisions. Be tactful when communicating our preferences.

TIP: It can be annoying when around someone who constantly overuses the word **"I"** word. *"I," "I," "I"!* The attention moves away from being purposeful or helpful to turning the spotlight on themselves. We get bored. Use personal experience and examples *purposefully* with an outcome in mind.

When "HOW" to Get It Done is Contested

There is more than one way to drill a hole.

We each have our preferences on <u>how</u> to get things done. We may both agree on the outcome and its importance *(what+why)*. However, **how** to get there is the point of contention. What makes my approach the best way to fulfill the task? When insisting, include strong and convincing reasons *why.*

Invite the other person's thoughts through *test questions* when a resistant attitude is present. *"What is your thinking around this idea?" "What are the advantages of doing it that way?" "What other alternatives have you considered?"* Our questions may awaken better methods, or we discover a hole in our own thinking.

When discussing, weigh the evidence and interests between all options. List the pros and cons of each idea and decide which will yield the best results. **When what+why and how are agreed upon, we move in the same direction with certainty and less friction.**

Occasionally we'll encounter someone with an unorthodox technique coupled with unwavering confidence, and unable to comprehend the thinking we encounter. Interests collide, thus get polarized by disparaging narratives. The situation could turn into a crisis over control, fighting over *who* is right. Even after discussion, both may still feel strongly that their way is still the best. Our choice is to give in, hold our ground, or go our separate ways.

TIP: When in a *position of power*, such as a parent or boss, asking questions becomes even more significant. We communicate, *"Your thoughts are important to me."* We instill trust and confidence in the relationship.

If we're saying to ourselves, "There is only <u>one</u> way, and it's my way," we are probably misguided.

Putting it All Together
What + Why + How

People do things for their reasons, not ours. - Dale Carnegie

The Action vs. The Effect

I burn my hand on a hot stove. Was it touching the stove *(the action)* **or** getting burned *(the effect)* that taught me? The memory of the burn lasts longer, reminding me of the cost of my action, especially when significant. We call this natural learning. To illuminate:

A mom and dad had been fighting all weekend. On Sunday night, the mom put her six-year-old daughter to bed when she heard, "You and daddy yell a lot." The mom explained that relationships are hard, and that she was too young to understand that fighting is part of it. The daughter looked at her mom with a bewildering stare.

How would this be different if the young daughter had instead said, *"Mommy, when I hear you and Daddy scream at each other, I get really scared and hide in the closet and cry."* If her daughter had said this, the next time the parents fight, they may be more mindful of the <u>effect</u> and <u>cost</u> of fighting on their daughter.

Change lasts when it comes through inspiration, not accusation. – Peggy Noonan

Tactfully Address Unacceptable Behavior
Using What + Why + How

What happens if we encounter unacceptable behavior. Sometimes we brush it aside as part of life and at other times it becomes too costly to ignore. How we address these issues can sway the outcome.

Below are three steps to discuss unwanted behavior respectfully and follow the principal of natural learning. **The three steps** include the *What, Why,* and *How.*

Step 1 Our frustration typically point to **WHAT** they *did* that's troubling us. *"You're always late to the meetings." "You're always leaving a mess around the house."* When critical, we provoke denial or excuses, which distances resolution. Instead, open by converting what they did into a specific positive outcome. *"I'd like for you to be on time for our meetings." "I would like the dirty clothes put in the hamper."*

Step 2 We want to resolve the cost and effects of their actions. In other words, **WHY** it's in both of our interests to find a solution. The conversation goes more smoothly when we concentrate on fixing the effects of those actions without criticism, blame, or judgment. Most are usually unaware of their behavior's impact on others and are more inclined to accommodate when they care about the inconvenience created.

When expressing the *"why,"* be <u>specific</u> with the *time* and *place* we last witnessed their behavior. When precise, we lead the receiver's mind to that moment, making our motive clear. It is hard to deny when we're accurate. Avoid using a general and vague time and place, which will lead to denial or justification. *"You <u>always</u> do that,"* or *"You <u>never</u> help out."* Impart two thoughts in Step 2: State the specific *action (when and where)* **and** follow with the *effects* of those actions. *"Taking a 35-minute shower this morning left the rest of us without hot water."*

<table><tr><td>**Step 3**</td><td>Express **HOW** we want the outcome to look. State as a direct statement; *"I need the report by 4 p.m.."* Or as a question, *"What needs to happen for the report to be*</td></tr></table>

done by 4 p.m.?", inviting their input or suggestions. To further induce, we can offer support by asking, *"What can I (or we) do to support this decision?"*

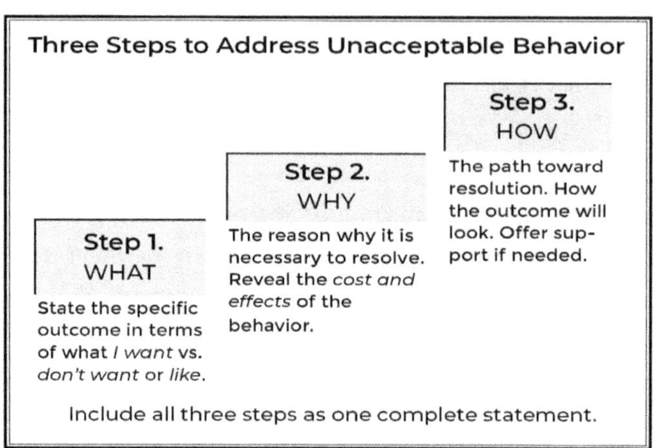

TIP: If we get resistance when using the three-step approach, ask: *"Is it in both (or all) of our best interests to resolve this?"*

Everyday Examples

The following examples are ways we can word the What+Why+ How for various scenarios. The initial statement shows how leading with our frustration may sound and the response it may yield.

Being Late

"Sarah, can't you ever be on time? You're <u>always</u> late to our meetings."
(Critical and opens up to excuses)

WHAT outcome I want: *I'd like for you to be on time for our meetings.*

WHY it is important: *Coming in late this morning interrupted the participants.*

HOW to be resolved: *What needs to happen for you to be on time for future meetings?*

Does Sarah want to disrupt her co-workers and the meeting? Are the *effects* (Why) inspiring enough for her to change her actions? If she does not care, a more significant problem lies underneath.

Leaving a Mess

"You <u>always</u> leave a mess wherever you go!" (Sounds judgmental)

WHAT outcome I want: *I'd like to see the dishes put in the kitchen when you're done eating.*

WHY it is important: *When I see dirty dinner plates left on the coffee table like this morning, I get irritated because I need order in the rooms we share.*

HOW to be resolved: *When you are done eating, would you take your dirty plates to the kitchen and place them in the dishwasher?*

Leading with our frustration puts people in an uncomfortable position. Calm down and think about the desired outcome. Instead of arguing over what they did, the three-step process moves our concerns toward a collaborative solution. Any agreement can be used as a future reminder.

Too Many Mistakes

"Can't you get that brochure right! Mistake after mistake!
Best you get your focus on target." (Sounds like a threat. Browbeaten)

WHAT outcome I want: *I need more accuracy on the brochure we mail out.*

WHY it is important: *I counted a dozen grammatical and spelling errors on the latest brochure, and I am frustrated because I want to present a professional image for our company.*

HOW to be resolved: *What needs to happen to have more accuracy from now on?*

Keeping Your Word

"Why didn't you come home when you said you would?"
(Invites a litany of excuses that does not resolve anything.)

WHAT outcome I want: *I would appreciate you coming home when you say you will.*

WHY it is important: *I was worried sick, hoping you were okay when you were out late last night. And when I called, your phone went to voicemail.*

HOW to be resolved: *What can we do to ensure you'll be home when you say you will?*

Chronic Complainer

"Can't you stop complaining about everything!
I don't want to hear it!" (Negating and Insensitive)

WHAT outcome I want: *I would rather hear solutions when you talk to me about a problem.*

WHY it is important: *When I hear complaints, I am unable to do anything. My time is valuable, and I'm powerless to support you without a possible solution.*

HOW to be resolved: *Please voice the possible solutions. Will that work for you?*

We make it easier to inspire improvement by tactfully addressing how their actions effect the world around them. Our goal is to find a solution to the problem without attacking and blaming. We are more open when we are not defending ourselves.

Using the What+Why+How problem-solving process works when there is a *difference in power* between parties. To illustrate:

Hal is the group leader for a small software company. He is responsible for managing the workflow between four software development teams. Deadlines were approaching to complete the final stages of a project. Rumors circulated that Hal had an affair with Samantha (a software engineer from one of the teams) that went awry.

In a meeting with Samantha and her five team members, it became evident to everyone that Hal was targeting Samantha with condemning questions and comments, embarrassing her in front of the group. Afterward, her team members asked her what was going on between them. She shrugged her shoulders and didn't reply. Samantha's team decided to address the issue directly with Hal, requesting a meeting. They figured they'd have strength in numbers, though Samantha stayed behind. Here is what was said:

WHAT outcome I want:	*Hal, we would like to see Samantha treated respectfully in the meetings.*
WHY it is important:	*During the meeting last Tuesday, our team member (Samantha) was being challenged and embarrassed in front of us for no apparent reason. This distraction is affecting our morale and productivity, and we're starting to feel resentful. Samantha is an integral part of our team.*
HOW to be resolved:	*We would like to see Samantha treated fairly, so we can get on with our work without distraction and meet the forthcoming deadline.*

Hal listened and concluded, *"There isn't a problem between us."* Hal now has a choice. Is the unresolved problem with Samantha worth the cost of lousy morale and lost productivity with deadlines approaching the project? It serves Hal's interest to resolve the issue because the price is too great.

At the next group meeting, the tone was completely different, and Samantha was no longer a target of Hal's inappropriate remarks. Appeal to people's interests to illustrate the cost of their unwelcome behavior.

The fastest way around a problem is through.

Chapter 16

Simplify Complex Ideas

It is a luxury to be understood. - Ralph Waldo Emerson

Quotes, analogies, and anecdotes can make complex ideas easier to grasp. We support our message in an alternative way. When properly used, we engage the listener's whole brain by including creative and colorful verbal comparisons. Instead of bombarding with fact after fact, sprinkle our message with any of these three creative threads to support our main point.

Analogies - Using Comparisons

One good analogy is worth three hours of discussion. - Dudley Malone

An analogy *(including similes and metaphors)* is a great way to make an unclear point, concept, or idea clear through comparison. We creatively draw a clever parallel from something vague or unknown to something commonly known. Analogies stir the listener's imagination while connecting to their literal brain.

Note: Despite subtle differences, I will use the word analogies to include *similes* and *metaphors*. They all hinge on comparisons. A simile is saying something *is like* something else. A metaphor is poetically saying something *is* something else.

Examples include:

In the early 1980s, Ronald Reagan illustrated the national debt by saying, *"How much is a trillion dollars? It's a stack of thousand-dollar bills sixty-seven miles high."*

"Having high cholesterol is like having hair that clogs your drain. It slows flow." We take one keyword whose definition we're trying to convey and compare it with something else commonly understood by the listener.

When Jerry Spence declined to be on the O.J. Simpson legal team, he said, *"Preparing a case is like a blank canvas. The more artists working on the same canvas, the messier the painting."*

The perils of personal debt can be explained with a comparison. *"Carrying large debt is like strapping a bag of concrete on your back. The first bag may not be too heavy, but each additional bag begins to weigh down your life."*

Arnold Schwarzenegger, then governor of California, was an advocate for renewable energy. He used a comparison to illustrate his argument in a very vivid way:

"There are two doors. Behind door number one is a completely sealed room with a regular, gasoline-fueled car. Behind door number two is an identical, completely sealed room with an electric car. Both engines are running full blast.

I want you to pick a door to open, enter the room, and shut the door behind you. You have to stay in the room you choose for one hour. You cannot turn off the engine. You do not get a gas mask.

Which door would you choose? I'm guessing you chose door number two with the electric car, right? This is the choice the world is making right now."

Anecdotes/Stories - Drawing on Personal Experiences

Storytelling reveals meaning
without committing the error of defining it. - Edward Abby

Ever lose interest listening to someone go on and on, fact after the fact trying to prove a point? We think to ourselves, *"Too much information! What are they trying to say?"* Those who take their time take ours. An anecdote is a brief, exciting, and amusing tale that sheds light on a specific point we're trying to exemplify. We draw upon an actual incident from our life or one we heard from someone else. We *do not* focus on ourselves. An anecdote concentrates on the point we are trying to make to our audience.

What's more compelling and influencing? I tell someone why they shouldn't shoot animals, or include a brief anecdote about a life lesson learned by shooting an animal to strengthen the point?

"My brother and I went camping in a remote logged area in the Cascades when I was young. The next morning I woke to the sound of dozens of birds chirping in a lone tree about thirty yards away. Not thinking, I took my .22 rifle and aimed at one of the birds. I shot, and the bird fell to the ground. The others scattered from the sound of the gunshot. The bird I hit was wounded, flapping its wings on the ground when the other birds returned to its aid. As I watched, I felt awful. I never used my rifle again. I learned the harm of fruitlessly killing animals from that experience and haven't done so since."

Our life is full of incidents that we can add to our conversations and presentations with purpose. Use real-life experiences that tie into our point. Elements of a good anecdote (story) are:

- Specific and interesting (One incident in time)
- Descriptive (Details add color)
- Action (Include verbs)
- Told from the first person (I or We instead of You language)
- End with a moral, point or lesson learned.

When sharing an anecdote, our story can be heard by many people and understood on their level of awareness. Because a good story is entertaining, people remember it far longer than a series of facts. How many stories do we remember hearing from our past that are still memorable today?

Life's experiences provide us a library of stories. Each story can teach, build trust, connect, and explain complex truths clearly. Use anecdotes to bridge gaps of understanding entertainingly in a memorable way.

Aphorisms/Quotes - Saying More with Less

I quote others only to better express myself. - Michel de Montaigne

Quotes (or aphorisms) are alternative ways to back up our point with humor or insight. My mentor would call quotes *"fast food wisdom."* We borrow from other's distilled wisdom and present them as a brief sentence or quip. Use a quote to illustrate, summarize, or support a point we are trying to make. Be selective. Pick a quote that fits our subject. Quotations add credibility to our message. When we quote someone famous, it seems like they're validating our idea.

Use quotes to entertain, educate, persuade, summarize, and as a resource for our presentations, social media, writings, or just for fun. Below are examples of the supportive quality of quotes:

When preparing a presentation, for example, recall aphorisms to remind ourselves to keep it short. *"One of the most important ingredients in a recipe of speaking is plenty of shortening." "I remember the lesson from the horse and buggy days. The longer the spoke, the bigger the tire."*

I've learned that people will forget what you said,
people will forget what you did,
but people will never forget how you made them feel. - Maya Angelou

√ **Communication defined:** The *effects* our words have on others.

√ When stating **WHAT** we want or know, **WHY** it is of value or instructions on **HOW** to do something, we impart our point of view *(perspective, priorities, bias, opinions, interests, wants, and desires)*. Thus, our statement can challenge the way others see things, which can quickly lead to misunderstanding and disagreement.

√ People hear more literally (without misconstruing) when we state *what they can do* **or** *what I want* versus *what they can't do* **or** *what I don't like.*

√ Using criticism to get what we want is <u>indirect</u> and invites justification instead of cooperation. We voice what they did—not what I want.

√ Misusing the twelve words risks pushing people's buttons.

√ When we encounter hesitancy or objections to our appeal or proposal, the reason *"why"* is often in question. **When we exclude** *"why"* with *"what we want,"* we leave the other person to draw their own conclusions about its importance.

√ Include the *"what"* plus the *"why"* to communicate the **purpose, benefit,** or **vision** behind our request. Make it easy for others to see how serving our interests serves theirs.

√ When explaining **HOW** to do something, give advice, state our view, or coach for improvement, draw from our personal experiences. **Our examples influence when they share the other person's interests.**

√ When *what+why* and *how* are agreed, we all move in the same direction with certainty and less friction.

Conclusion

We are living in the more complex world of the twenty-first century. Overwhelming options, information, and distractions can stress our daily interactions. Disagreements are likely to arise, and at times move into an argument.

Emotions complicate the matter. When debate occurs, our instinct is to protect our version, which may challenge the other person's view. We do not all think alike. Communication works, until it doesn't. When it doesn't, a mature approach to communication is necessary—knowing what to listen for, expressing ourselves in a manner to be heard, learning how to redirect tension back into a civil discussion, and when to walk away.

The language and skills in this book acknowledge three core human needs that reduce the chance of contention:

- Honoring one's dignity with respect.

- Understanding the role of self-interest.

- Accepting people's need to be heard.

When properly applied, the *A.C.T. Way to Respond* affirms all three needs to everyone's benefit. The hardest part will be learning to get past our unfruitful ways of reacting.

My hope is this concise handbook becomes the *"go-to"* resource to help us prepare before an important meeting or proposal. Also, to learn the many ways of responding to delicate conversations in our daily interactions, whether written or spoken. We can then present our words with purpose, clarity, and confidence.

It's not WHAT we say, It's HOW we say it!

Appendix

Values Exercise

*When your values are clear to you,
making decisions becomes easier.* - Roy E. Disney

Review the list of forty-five values and needs. Prioritize the top ten most instrumental in shaping your life. There are hundreds of values and needs. Include any not listed. The **definition** and **importance** we place on each personal value vary from person to person. We may both want *loyalty* yet differ in how we define it, and how it is best supported. Each value and need has a meaning and story that invites our curiosity.

Common Values and Needs

Achievement	Fairness	Personal Growth
Adventure	Flexibility	Privacy
Ambition	Freedom	Punctuality
Closeness	Frugality/Economy	Recognition
Calmness	Genuineness	Reliability
Commitment	Gratitude	Respect/Dignity
Competence	Harmony	Routine
Comfort	Honesty	Safety/Security
Competition	Hygiene	Spirituality
Conformity	Independence	Stability
Cooperation	Intimacy	Structure
Curiosity	Integrity	Support
Dependability	Kindness	Teamwork
Directness	Loyalty	Trustworthiness
Equality	Order	Variety

Four questions about our values and needs:

- How do my values prioritize my decisions in life?
- How do my values influence my interactions with others?
- What role do my values play in disagreements I encounter?
- What behaviors and actions in others violate my values at home and work?

Share our list of values and needs with those close to us. Ask them to rank their top ten. Then, compare and discuss variations and how they play out in our relationship.

Great Questions and Their Uses

Define the Situation

- *What does that look like to you? How do you define...?*

- *What actions let you know that is being honored and supported?*

- *Tell me more about that?*

- *How do you see the situation?*

- *What led you to believe this? (Instead of asking "WHY" question)*

- *Paint me a picture of how you'd like it to be?*

- *What are you not getting that you are wanting?*

- *If you were me, what would you do?*

The Cost of a Decision

- *How do you see this affecting our relationship / department / children . . .?*

- *Who else is being affected by this?*

- *Is this what we want?*

- *If this continues, then what?*

Follow-up on a Decision

- *When was a time it did work? How is it different now?*

- *What will this look like six months from now?*

- *In addition to your idea, what else might work?*

- *What if we were to...?*

- *Is there another way of looking at this?*

- *What can we do to insure that both of our needs are satisfied?*

- *What is it you heard me say?*

- *What do you like most and least about the decision?*

Test the Thinking and Flexibility of a Response

- *Is there another way to look at this?*

- *Is that your final answer?*

- *What if I'm unable to do that? Then what?*

- *What would happen if we tried ...?*

- *What other possibilities should we consider?*

- *When you said _______, what did you mean?*

- *How does this satisfy my needs?*

- *How is that going to help you get what you want?*

- *What about what's important to me?*

Examples of Follow-up Questions

"How do you mean?"
"What makes you say that?"
"What led to that conclusion?"
"Why is that?"
"What does that look like to you?"
"How do you define...?"
"How do you see the situation."
"Why do you think that is so?"
"How do you wish it was?"
"How would you like to see it fixed?"
"How do we move forward?"
"What makes that important to you?"
"Is that realistic?"
"How so?"
"And?"
"Because?"
"For example?"
"Which means?"
"Then what?"
"In what way?"
"Such as?"

Examples of the A.C.T. in Everyday Life

Appendix 3 will introduce various life scenarios on how to creatively and skillfully apply the A.C.T. Way to respond without argument.

The A.C.T. Way to Respond to Everyday Communication Without Argument

Acknowledge   Clarify   Talk

Emotional ➝ Conversational

Emotional Zone	**Discovery Zone**	**Discussion Zone**
Calm emotions by validating their experience to let them know they were heard.	Ask the right question to clarify their view before sharing ours.	Talk it out and work towards a solution. (What + Why + How)

Strong emotions compromise the ability to reason and listen.

Copyright © 2021 Mark Ortman

Following are a collection of nine stories and anecdotes shared or witnessed.

Instead of Defending

When my husband, children, or co-workers say uncomfortable things to me (criticisms, blame, judgments), my knee-jerk response was defensive, which went nowhere except to a time-wasting argument. I realized that defending my feelings worsened the situation. Now I do the opposite with far better results. I express my internal experience without judgment—an acknowledgment in reverse. I then follow with a question. I might respond to an uncomfortable comment, *"That comment hurts me. Is that what you want?" "I'm feeling attacked. Is that going to help you get what you want?"* I appeal to their sense of self-respect and self-interest. More often than not, they cool down and become conscious of what they did. Now an honest conversation can occur. Acknowledging (**A**) in reverse, stating my experience in the first person instead of defending, followed by a question to Clarify (**C**), is quite powerful for others to hear.

The Miracle Manager

Three weeks into my first job after college, the executive assistant comes to me and says, *"Jim (my manager) would like to see you in his office."* My immediate thought was, *"Oh boy, what did I do?"* I silently followed the executive assistant to Jim's office. He greeted me with a smile and acknowledgment, *"Mark, I hear great things from the vendors about your marketing project! We haven't had a chance to talk with my travel schedule and would like to spend a little time to get caught up."* I sat and immediately calmed down as we chatted informally. Then he said, *"Something I ask each of my new team members is, how do you best like to be managed?"* I thought to myself, *"That is an unusual request."* I answered, and he wrote down my response, clarifying each point. Guess how he managed me? Yes, the way we agreed. Jim's Acknowledgment (**A**) and Clarifying (**C**) questions opened the door to honest Talk (**T**). I felt important to participate in how I was to be managed.

Mom Visits

My mom is coming to visit. I'm excited yet apprehensive about her critical and controlling nature. Her favorite phrases are; *"You should..."* and *"Why did you...?"* Day three into her visit, her old habit surfaced. She didn't like the way I cooked dinner. She said, *"Why didn't you follow the directions? You never follow the directions!"* It sure sounded like shame and criticism to me. Instead of the old patterns of defending myself, I held my buttons at bay and Acknowledged (**A**) and asked a question to Clarify (**C**). *"I'm so sorry you didn't enjoy the meal, Mom. Would you like to cook dinner tomorrow night?"* Mom went silent, then apologized. She may not change her nature, though she may think twice before judging me if I continue to respond skillfully and respectfully. She may not change, yet I can.

Micromanaged

I work for a micromanager. When given a task, I can feel Elise looking over my shoulder, providing unsolicited advice along the way. I get the sense I'm not trusted. I work best on my own. I'm smart enough to correct my mistakes and not afraid to ask for help when needed. Working at my capacity is difficult. I'm always on edge, and it is affecting my attitude.

Fed up, I mustered the courage to meet and discuss this matter. I could approach leading with my frustration labeling what Elise does, or I could open with a resolving question in the direction I want to go. *"Elise, would you be interested in finding a way to get the most productive work out of me?"* She replies, *"Of course!"* I reversed the question, which allowed me to answer instead of her responding.

I described what I wanted, *"I work best independently as long as I have a clear picture of the vision."* I clarified without accusation. *"I want to support your vision with the right detail. It's important for me to work on my own. I can agree to periodic check-ins."* I was conscious of not being critical or using the word *"micromanage."* I used positive words she could hear and shared how I work best. *"I pride myself in my independence and work most productively when I have some free reigns. Will that work for you?"* We discussed back and forth how to make that happen within her comfort zone. Not everyone treats us the way we want. I was opening a discussion to let Elise know how to treat me best within negotiable terms! Good luck trying to change people. Our best shot is showing how to treat us to get the best results.

Putting a Problem in Perspective with Questions

The film composer meets with the director to review the music produced for an upcoming TV series. They sit together and watch the first episode with the new music playing in the background.

Composer: *"What do you think?"*
Director: *"I hate the music for that scene!"*

Composer: *"What do you hate about it?"*
Director: *"It's not exactly what I want."*

Composer: *"How do you mean?"* They listen again to the piece.
Director: *"The strings are too loud."*

Composer: *"Oh, I can easily fix that."*
Director: *"Great! It's a go."*

Perceptions can sometimes magnify a problem until we understand through questions what is behind the concern.

New to the Department

Hannah temporarily transfers into a short-staffed department. She met with her lead to go over responsibilities. He stressed the value of teamwork. She followed with, *"What does good teamwork look like to you?"* He openly answered, and she followed up with more questions to clarify. Now it's clear how to fit in and work within the new department.

Arguing to Get My Way

Dale would argue with anyone to get his way. One day I asked, *"Why do you argue?"* He said, *"Because I'm right."* "Oh, come on, Dale," I exclaimed. He replied, *"I usually get what I want when I raise my voice."* His honest response led me to ask, *"If that didn't work, what would you do?"* He responded, *"I'd have to find another way."* People adjust to meet their interests and needs.

Job Interview

I was very nervous going into the job interview, and I decided to do something different. I prepared by researching the company and learning their strengths and differences from competitors. Instead of immediately being put on the spot with questions, I decided to ask questions first. I walked into the interview room and asked to take a seat. I acknowledged **(A)**, *"Thanks for the opportunity to interview. I've read how your new product break-through will lead the industry moving forward."* The interviewer looked at me with an unexpected smile. I followed with a question to Clarify **(C)**, *"What led you to work here?"* She briefly told me her story. I followed with one more question. *"What do you like most about working here?"* I felt at ease and it only took a few minutes for us to connect. Our meeting felt more like a conversation than an interview.

Negotiating with My Teenager

One wise parent shared with me how he negotiates with his sixteen-year-old son staying out late. *"Alex does not have a car yet, so we let him use ours on weekends. He often asks to stay out later than is comfortable for us. Alex wants to stay out until 1:00 a.m. I tell him he can stay out until 1:00 a.m., except the car has a curfew of 11 p.m. If he does not bring the car back at curfew, he knows he risks losing car privileges. Rarely does he go back out after returning the car. Once in a while, I will extend the car curfew on special occasions. I've found this to be an effective way to negotiate with my son. He realizes there are consequences to his actions and agreements. As we begin to treat our teens as the adults they are becoming, the sooner they may embrace the responsibilities of adulthood. A lesson I feel is important and want to instill."*

Let us be kinder to one another. - Aldous Huxley's last words

About the Author

Mark Ortman's curious and inspiring nature extends more than three and a half decades in the field of communication as a coach, mediator, and trainer. His Master's degree is from the University of Denver in Communication. He was awarded ten national instructional awards and certified as a mediator along his journey.

Mark listened to more than 24,000 stories from clients and students during his career, disclosing what works and what doesn't in daily interactions. His first book, *Now That Makes Sense*, compiles a collection of quotations and insights around communication, human relations, and human nature. Ortman's sixth book, *The Secret to Everyday Communication*, reveals the language and words that move disagreements into a discussion without argument.

Ortman's previous titles include: *So Many Ways to Say Thank You* (1993), *A Simple Guide to Self-Publishing* (1994), *The Teachers Book of Wit* (1996), and *A Simple Guide to Marketing Your Book* (1998).

Mark composes electronic music in his home studio with four albums to date: *Wednesday's Dream* (1993), *Journey's* (2014), *Voices From The Sea* (2017), and *Strange Occurences* (2020). He can be reached at: mark@markortman.com

* * *

Order Book

The Secret to Everyday Communication *(Without Argument)*. Everyday Communication works, until it doesn't. When emotions escalate, talk can quickly turn into an argument. Whether at home or at work, the three skills presented in this book share powerful techniques to defuse, clarify, and discuss differences when they arise.

ISBN: 978-0-9634699-2-2 / 6x9 / 112 pages
Released 2022

$15.95 US

Now That Makes Sense! Relating to People with Wit & Wisdom. An entertaining resource of 750 of history's most brilliant saying around communication, human relations, and human nature. Use this book to entertain, educate, persuade and as a resource for your blog, writings, newsletter, social media, or presentations.

ISBN: 978-0-9634699-9-1 / 5.5x8.5 / 99 pages
Revised Edition 2019

$15.00 US

Available where books are sold.

Quantity discounts available through the publisher.